STOP the violence!

PRAISE FOR *STOP THE VIOLENCE!* BY WENDY MORRIS

"This curriculum is a wide-reaching resource, breaking new ground in the critical issues surrounding violence and youth. It is a must for all of us struggling to help youth and adults create a violence-free world."

—Jim and Kathy McGinnis
Directors, Institute for Peace and Justice

"A creative curriculum that combines in-depth analysis of violence in our culture with excellent biblical resources and contemporary case studies. The result is a rare, experiential study resource for congregations and communities working for a non-violent society."

—Richard Tholin
Senior Scholar in Christian Social Ethics
and retired Academic Dean
Garrett-Evangelical Theological Seminary
Evanston, Illinois

"Having worked 27 years with active gang members and other ex-prisoners, we feel greatly encouraged by reviewing this curriculum. We are pleased to know that faith-based organizations are getting involved in reclaiming our young people. This curriculum is 'required reading' for all those organizations working with challenged youth."

—Nancy Jackson
Executive Director, Prologue, Inc.,
which operates three alternative high schools
and a charter school

"This is a ground-breaking contribution to faith-based communities that are interested in knowing what to do about the critical issue of violence in the U.S. culture. Written in an approachable style, this curriculum attempts to build upon the strengths of each group and challenges them to do something that will make a difference in their immediate area. This guide helps faith-based groups in these confusing and complex times."

—*Cecelia M. Long*
General Secretariat
United Methodist Church

"I highly recommend *Stop the Violence!* to teachers, youth ministers, and church and community leaders as a practical, well-designed program addressing our violent society and its impact on youth. Ms. Morris's deep respect for and understanding and love of children and youth permeates each chapter. May this resource be widely used and produce meaningful discussions that empower youth to use their gifts and help transform U.S. society."

—*Joyce Ruhaak*
Parish Outreach Coordinator
Peace & Justice Ministry
Catholic Diocese of Joliet, Illinois

"With violence in our schools, our neighborhoods, our very homes, so many of us feel overwhelmed and helpless. This book confronts despair and gives real hope for how we might deal with this critical problem—an issue which touches the life of every American. Ms. Morris gives thoughtful, concrete, and realistic ways to *Stop the Violence!* I highly recommend this book to anyone who cares about our children, our youth, our people."

—*Rev. Sam Leonard*
Alban Consultant

STOP the violence!

educating ourselves to protect our youth

LEADER'S GUIDE

wilda k. w. morris

Foreword by Tony Campolo

Judson Press
Valley Forge

Stop the Violence!
Educating Ourselves to Protect Our Youth
Leader's Guide
ISBN 0-8170-1386-5
© 2001 by Judson Press, Valley Forge, PA 19482–0851
All rights reserved.

Printed in the U.S.A.
07 06 05 04 03 02 01
10 9 8 7 6 5 4 3 2 1

CONTENTS

FOREWORD

The massacre at Columbine High School in the suburbs of Denver, Colorado, stunned and grieved the nation. The news stories and statistics concerning youth violence are frightening, that children so young are capable of so much rage, so much bloodshed. Our first inclination may be to ask how we can protect ourselves against them. But, the Christian must ask a deeper question: "How can we save them from self destruction?"

Stop the Violence! is about many things, but primarily it is about how people—especially church people—can become a dynamic force in addressing the violence of teenagers and exercise a transforming influence in their lives. As the church struggles to understand violent young people, the most basic reasons for their antisocial behavior do not require extensive studies by sociologists.

When the typical church member is asked about causes for violence among youth, the answer likely to be forthcoming is "the breakdown of the family." Divorce has become an epidemic in our society, such that half of the children being raised in America today are being raised with at least one parent absent from the home. Studies will reveal what we all know—that children raised apart from intact families have a significantly greater propensity for becoming violent criminals than those who are raised in intact families.

Even setting aside the statistics on divorced families, we face the staggering incidence of premarital pregnancies. Approximately one-third of all the children born in America these days have been born out of wedlock, and the statistic is even higher in places where urban disintegration is most evident. These children are likely to be raised by mothers in their early teens who live in conditions of extreme poverty, and who have little support or knowledge when it comes to child-raising practices. Children raised without strong parental images will be prone to struggle in establishing their own identities, and often they will join gangs simply because a gang gives them a source of self-identity.

Youth often feel powerless to control their own destinies. In a world in which personal achievement is expected from every citizen, young people—especially impoverished youth—experience extreme frustration because they are convinced that they lack the capacity to be successful. They sense that they are failing at school and that they will never have the skills that success requires. They are also aware that they lack the network of friends and relatives who can get them interviews and pave the way for employment opportunities. In many instances they feel the impact of racial discrimination and have developed a victim mentality that is buttressed by the realities of what they experience in everyday life. Such hurting, disaffected people can become dangerous. The slightest evidence of disrespect is prone to elicit violence in these individuals. In most urban neighborhoods, violent young people explain that they were "dissed" (disrespected) by the person that was shot or beaten up. The seething anger that lies beneath the surface of a significant proportion of urban youth provides the nitroglycerin for explosive behavior. Churches and other community groups need to address these emotional dispositions by providing positive avenues for establishing wholesome identities and a sense of community.

It is not enough for these at-risk young people to attend some seminar where they are urged to yell, "I am somebody!" They know that they get respect only if they do things that are respected, and they feel that they lack the opportunity for such achievements. Their sensitivity to being at the bottom of the socioeconomic system and to the feeling that others look down on them because of their low status gives rise to anger that can flare at the most minute slight by a school teacher or by a passerby on the sidewalk.

I want to acknowledge that poverty and youth violence are not confined to urban America. Almost half of all children living below the poverty level reside in rural areas, such as Appalachia. We also face growing concerns about suburban young people—children and teens who are growing up in middle-class America with all of the advantages that should make their future success guaranteed. Instead, shoplifting by teenagers has become endemic in many suburban shopping malls, and the malls themselves have become places where a new breed of suburban gangs is beginning to coalesce. And of course, the massacre in Columbine and other eruptions of violence in suburban and rural settings make it clear that urban teens are not the only ones at risk for becoming the perpetrators and victims of youth violence. This book will go a long way in directing churches and concerned communities concerning youth violence in neighborhoods all across America.

The question that arises is whether or not the church in particular is ready to provide a community of loving acceptance that affirms the worth of otherwise demoralized youth. Author Wendy Morris believes that we can—and must, and I am convinced that she is right. When functioning in its most Christlike capacity, the church is an affirming fellowship of believers, and if it knows how to extend that spirit of community among the poor, the oppressed, the displaced, and the marginalized, it can fulfill a God-given mission in our troubled times.

Stop the Violence! gets the church (and other community organizations) moving in the right direction. It is an attempt to compel all of us in the household of faith to begin asking the right questions and exploring options for action. This book is full of hope, as well it should be, because if we are truly the people with Good News for today's world, we must be a people of hope.

A few years ago, a gang summit was held in Kansas City, Missouri. Hundreds of gang leaders responded to the invitation and gathered to discuss ways that they might move into more constructive life styles. In the midst of discussion, one young man stood and shouted to the organizers of the summit, "You just don't get it! We need God!" Indeed, those who had called the summit didn't get it. For beyond all the sociological solutions to the gang problem, young people need to come into a personal relationship with Jesus Christ. Conversion, in the old-fashioned sense of the word, is an absolute necessity. For unless young people are empowered by the Spirit of God, they will lack the strength and the vision essential to surmount the troublesome social forces that they find in their everyday lives. The odds are against most children and youth who grow up in volatile families or who live in at-risk neighborhoods. But, if the Holy Spirit is in them, these forces cannot overcome them. It is essential for the church to become involved with the problems of troubled youth, because for many, if not for most, only personal conversion can lead to them having the will and the strength to be victors over their existential situation.

Tony Campolo, Ph.D.
Eastern College
St. Davids, Pennsylvania

INTRODUCTION

YOUR INTEREST IN THE STUDY OF YOUTH VIOLENCE

If you have this book in your hand, it is likely that you are considering facilitating a study of youth violence. Perhaps you have already made a commitment to do so. This suggests that you are concerned about and committed to taking action to protect children and youth. Stop and respond to the questions below. If you are helping to facilitate this study with a group, discuss these questions with your cofacilitator(s) when you get together to plan.

☐ My feelings about facilitating or cofacilitating this study are

☐ What I would most like to get out of this experience is

☐ My feelings about working with my cofacilitators are

☐ What I would like to have happen as a result of this study is

Because of the breadth of different experiences that may motivate an interest in youth violence and gangs, people may come to this study with strong feelings, such as anger, grief, fear, curiosity, hopelessness, or despair. It is good to recognize those feelings in yourself and others.

The Participant's Book suggests some possible sources of interest in this issue. Please read the Introduction to the Participant's Book now if you have not already done so. Fill in your answers to questions in the boxes.

WHY THIS STUDY?

This curriculum provides an action/reflection process to help congregations and other groups learn about issues of youth violence and gangs and to decide whether and how to become involved. Involvement may include healing from violence, advocacy for children and youth and for social justice, prevention of violence, and/or intervention with gang-involved youth.

The curriculum addresses five primary concerns from a theological and sociological perspective: (1) reasons why rates of youth violence are so high and why youth gangs exist; (2) ways children and youth are often dehumanized in the U.S.; (3) the impact of youth violence on youth and on the larger community; (4) the relationship between social issues such as poverty and racism, on the one hand, and gangs and youth violence on the other; and (5) the development of constructive alternatives to youth violence and negative gang activities.

APPROACHES TO THE ISSUES OF YOUTH VIOLENCE AND GANGS

There are many approaches that can be taken to youth violence. In the Introduction to the Participant's Book and in Resource 2 you will find definitions and examples of four constructive approaches from which individuals and groups can select as they seek to use their gifts to help make life better, safer, and more wholesome for children and youth and for the communities in which they live.

WHO WILL USE THIS BOOK?

The curriculum will be used primarily by congregations or clusters of congregations and by community groups interested in the wellbeing of youth. It will be of interest to anyone concerned with either the negative impact of violence on young people and communities, or—more generally—on the plight of children and youth in the U.S. It includes resources and guidelines for adaptation for interfaith groups and partnerships that include representatives of both religious and secular groups.

Since issues of youth violence impact strongly on young people, we highly recommend that high school students and adults study this material together. In mixed-age groups, it is especially important that adults listen carefully to what the youth say and resist the temptation to dominate conversation and decision making. High school students often have information that few adults have concerning violence and gangs in their communities! Who knows better the interests—if not the needs—of teenagers? Who is more likely to know whether drugs are easily available in your community and whether or not young people bring guns to school?

Partnership

Some communities of faith or other organizations will work alone, while some will want to partner with other congregations or community organizations. Partnerships are recommended because they bring a variety of resources together and can thus be more effective.

If initially you do not find enough support in your congregation for partnering with others, use the session plans with your own group. By the end of the study, group members can reevaluate whether or not to enter into partnership. As you use action plans associated with each session, you will have opportunities to identify community organizations whose approach you find acceptable. You may recommend that other groups purchase this material to prepare for working together on the issue of youth violence.

We encourage you to think seriously about organizations in your neighborhood to see who has been left out and whose perspectives need to be heard. Often young people, those who are poor, or who are not white have more difficulty than others getting their viewpoints taken seriously. You can help make it possible for members of these groups to be heard.

Although we encourage you to be wary of groups or individuals whose main intention is punitive (e.g., to wipe out gangs and lock up gang members or to get all youth who have done or said anything violent "put away" for life), we are hopeful that working through the sessions in this book will help such persons reevaluate their position and become more constructive.

Recruitment of Participants

You as a facilitator and the congregation or organization you represent will need to decide whether your focus in recruitment will be on getting as many participants as possible or on getting participants with the highest level of commitment. If you succeed in recruiting people who are really committed to working toward reducing youth violence, it is more likely that you and those with whom you work will take significant action and really make a difference. Yet, the more people who become committed, the more effective your actions will be. Some persons may enter the study without a deep commitment but become committed as a result of what they learn. How you will balance these dynamics will depend to some extent on your local situation.

If the study is held during the regular church-school hour, you probably will have more participants, but many of them may not be committed to action on the issue of youth violence. If you schedule ten (or eleven) 2½-hour sessions or undertake the study during intensive weekend sessions, you may have fewer—but more committed—participants. The longer sessions will allow you to reach greater depth in your study.

You will especially want to encourage those who work with young people—from children through high school—to participate.

Facilitators in the Action-Reflection Approach to Learning

We recommend that the group have two or three cofacilitators. Cofacilitators should represent some of the diversity of the group. A teen and an adult could facilitate together. If the group is ethnically diverse, that diversity should be reflected in the leadership. If churches, synagogues and mosques are working together, an interfaith leadership team is needed. If two or more groups study the material together, the leadership team must not all come from one group. The facilitators should model cooperative, respectful partnership.

Facilitators should set an atmosphere in which everyone can share openly. This requires that participants feel safe from personal attack and believe they are being taken seriously. It is important to be gentle when challenging persons to consider new viewpoints. It may be helpful to return to the Guidelines for Discussion during later sessions if discussions get too heated.

Facilitators should read through the Participant's Book and Leader's Guide in their entirety before planning the sessions. This will give you a sense of where you are going and alert you to the need for advance preparation, such as the ordering of a video, and so on.

It may be possible for your group or a cluster of groups to arrange to train facilitators. To inquire about this possibility, call Wendy Morris at 630-739-2983, or write to her at 499 Falcon Ridge Way, Bolingbrook, Illinois 60440.

THE PRE-SESSION

We have provided for a "pre-session"—a single session that can be used in advance of the full-scale study—as a recruitment tool. It covers the important material in the Introduction to the Participant's Book. The pre-session provides potential participants an opportunity to experience the action-reflection model of learning and to consider making a commitment to the entire study.

Those who attend the pre-session and want to commit to the study can decide on a schedule for future sessions. This helps avoid scheduling conflicts. If you are working in a partnership, the group may also determine the locations for subsequent sessions. Those who attend the pre-session may help recruit friends and acquaintances.

If you are in a partnership, this pre-session is an opportunity to relieve

About the Sessions

☐ Sessions are planned step by step for those who want everything planned for them but can be adapted to meet the needs of particular groups and communities.

☐ Chairs should be placed in a circle so that everyone can see everyone else.

☐ We recommend that high school youth and adults participate together in these sessions.

☐ It is best to have two or three cofacilitators who may be of different ethnic backgrounds, from different congregations or groups that are studying the material cooperatively, and/or different age categories. The cofacilitators should plan together and divide leadership responsibilities equitably in order to model working together across ethnic and/or age lines.

anxiety by demonstrating sensitivity to the concerns of each group. Because the curriculum is published by a Christian publisher, it is assumed that the majority of users will be Christian. Consequently, each session includes a reflection on a Scripture passage from the Christian Bible. There is material concerning these texts in the Participant's Book and in the Leader's Guide, so it will be quite important to be sensitive to the concerns of participants of other faiths. This Leader's Guide provides suggestions on how to work together across these lines. A pre-session that demonstrates this sensitivity can assure those who are not Christian that they are full partners in the study and in the actions that follow.

DESCRIPTION OF SESSIONS

If you use the sessions as designed, each session will include:

☐ A Check-in at the beginning. Participants will need opportunities to process ideas they think of between sessions, their reading, and relevant news items, as well as the action steps they have taken. This is a time for getting in touch with the ideas and experiences participants bring to the sessions

☐ Reflection on a text from Scripture or other source as it relates to issues being studied

☐ New information on the topic

☐ An Action Plan suggesting things participants can do before the next session which will enrich the study

☐ A Closing that includes prayer or in some other way refocuses the attention of the group before participants depart

Scheduling of Sessions and Adapting Session Plans

The Session Outlines are written so they can be used in a variety of formats. The preferred pattern is to have ten (eleven with the pre-session) 2½–hour sessions. However, the material may be used in a religious education class or other group in ten to twenty 1–hour or 1½–hour sessions. Often such classes are organized in thirteen-week quarters. The material from one session plan could be split into two sessions, using the usual class time and adding a 1½–hour midweek session to cover the remainder of the material. The material would be covered in ten weeks, leaving three more weeks for additional planning of action steps, recruitment of persons to be involved in the ministries planned as a result of the study, and so on.

The material is organized so that it can be used during thirteen 1–hour sessions, but participants will not get the full benefit of the material. *If this material is covered in just thirteen 1–hour sessions, it is important to devote two sessions each to sessions six, eight, and ten.*

The material can be used in intensive weekend sessions, scheduled for two two-day weekends or a three-day weekend. However, we recommend that your group schedule ten 2½–hour sessions especially for this study. If the group or congregation is going to take the issue of youth violence seriously enough to take significant action, a high level of commitment is needed. If you schedule ten 2½–hour sessions, participants could consider it something like taking a course from the community college—with "homework" but without exams! A group with this level of commitment is much more likely to accomplish something important.

You will be more likely to recruit a large enough group with this degree of commitment if you work ecumenically. Some local businesses, schools, youth programs, or not-for-profit organizations may be interested in sending some of their staff to participate, counting the hours involved in the sessions (and time spent on Action Plans) as work hours or in-service training.

If your congregation or group opts for ten 2½–hour sessions (not counting the pre-session), you can follow the session plans as they are laid out in this manual. The activities that can most readily be omitted are marked as optional. Facilitators, of course, can select the components they think most helpful for their own group.

Time estimates are given as a range (e.g., 15–35 minutes). How long you will invest in a particular activity or discussion depends on the number of participants, the length of your session, and the needs and interests of your group. You may give the maximum recommended time to one activity and the minimum recommended time to another. Minimum time estimates generally add up to 60 minutes; maximum estimates add up to at least 2½ hours. In some cases they add up to more than 2½ hours, on the assumption that the facilitator will decide how much time to give certain activities or let the flow of the session be the determining factor. Just be certain to leave adequate time for the Action Plan portion of the session.

If you use these session plans during the time you usually have a religious education class, remember that there is a lot to cover. Encourage group members to make a commitment to be on time, attend every session, and get right to work.

If there are persons in your group who are not able to read well, this will require sensitivity and flexibility. Some information that participants might otherwise derive from their books can be read aloud. When directions suggest asking participants to read silently, ask for a volunteer to read aloud. When small groups are using written material, make sure each group includes someone who is willing to read aloud.

In interfaith groups, take turns selecting stories from your tradition that raise similar issues to the biblical texts in the session plans. Each faith has its own rich store of texts. If the group is largely "secular," you may use folk tales, news items, poems (such as the one in Session 1), or passages from various books that will stimulate reflection on the relevant issues.

Action Plans—Will My Group Do Them?

Action plans will provide your group with more information about (1) youth violence in your community or state, (2) programs for children and youth, and (3) local attitudes. They will provide you with more up to date information than most printed resources can. They are designed to draw participants into involvement in the issue of youth violence in a nonthreatening way, thus making it more likely that they will take significant action.

Some participants will get excited about Action Plans and find them the most helpful and challenging part of the study. Others will resist involvement. Some will find it difficult, due to transportation, health, and so on, to participate in some suggested actions. Few persons will participate in action plans after every session. Accept each person where he or she is, but encourage participation. Persons in your group may come up with alternate ideas for action plans especially suitable for use in your community. Go with those plans if they seem helpful.

Some action plans provide "Internet Options." Group members already "surfing the Net" might team up with others who haven't had that opportunity, as they search for information or send email messages to public officials. This may provide an opportunity for adults who don't know much about the Internet to learn from young people! If no one in your group is online, use the library as your resource for these action plans, if it is connected. Encourage each participant to be involved in at least one Internet Option if possible, but do not allow Internet options to replace the other Action Plan options.

We have provided Internet addresses for websites, but don't be discouraged if those sites or their addresses have changed, and the instructions don't quite work. If the site is still available, explore the current material that it presents. If not, use a search engine to look for something equivalent. Teens in your group or your public librarian may teach others how to do this.

The sessions outlined in this manual can be studied without doing Action Plans, but the study will be greatly enriched if group members work on Action Plans as often as possible. If your group does many of the Action Plans, by the end of the study, you will know your community better, be able to access information on important social issues, and be better prepared to make decisions about what you can do as individuals and as a group.

You may want to ask for volunteers to be media scouts, clipping articles from newspapers and magazines or reporting on TV or radio stories related to this study. A person in the group who cannot participate in action plans or a person who is shut-in might feel honored to be asked to take on this task. The role of media scout might be rotated weekly. Those who are shut-in may also be prayer partners.

The Group Binder and Clipping File

We recommend using a 2 or 3–inch-thick binder and a three-hole punch to hold paperwork for your group. Whenever a member takes notes on an interview, prepares a written report on some aspect of an Action Plan, or writes notes about or reviews books relevant to this study, a copy should be punched and put in the Group Binder. The binder should be available to group members when they want to refer to it. You may need additional binders before you complete this study. You may want to take pictures of group sessions and Action Plan activities to include in the binder. Media scouts can contribute newspaper clippings and notes from TV and radio reports.

The Group Binder will become a record of significant work done by the group and individual members of it. By gathering the materials together, you will make it easy for participants to review and celebrate what they have done. It can also be displayed for the congregation or other organizations interested in the work of the group.

These Are the Breaks

We highly recommend that you order "These Are the Breaks," a table game designed for use with Session 7. You should order well in advance by contacting the author at 499 Falcon Ridge Way, Bolingbrook, Illinois 60440, via telephone at 630-739-2983, or e-mail at wem@ameritech.net. Order one set for each four to six players, depending on the size of the tables you will be using. Or you may borrow the game from the Resource Center of the Northern Illinois Conference of the United Methodist Church (see address below under Video Options) for the cost of postage and handling.

Supplementary Books

There are a number of books and articles that would be excellent supplementary readings for this study. Several are recommended on pages 8–9 of the Participant's Book. In Session 1, you will be encouraged to find one or more persons to read a book and prepare to share information they learn from it as the sessions proceed. If your budget allows, you may purchase copies for the congregation or group. If your public library does not have the recommended books, they may be willing to purchase them or borrow them for you through interlibrary loan.

Video Options

There are video options included in several sessions. Facilitators will need to read these sessions well ahead of time and decide whether or not to use the videos. If you decide to use them, you may

☐ Try to find copies locally (through the state university video center, your denominational resource center, or a local library)

☐ Borrow a copy from the Media Resource Librarian, Northern Illinois Conference, United Methodist Church, 8765 W. Higgins Road, Suite 659, Chicago, Illinois 60631, telephone 773-380-5060, ext. 238; fax 773-380-5067 (depending on availability) for the cost of postage and handling.

☐ Purchase a copy for your own organization.

There are advantages to purchasing your own copies of videos, if you can afford to do so. Those who miss a session in which a video is shown could borrow it to watch at home (give them the discussion questions to ponder in the process), and persons who want to review information in the video could do so. Purchase prices are subject to change.

Ordering Information

Warning Signs: A Look at Teenage Violence (Session 2 alternative if you cannot have teenagers present for the session): 23–minute video highlighting four teens who have been affected by violence and exploring sources and symptoms of violence and ways to prevent it. It can be purchased from Meridian Education Corporation, 236 East Front Street, Bloomington, Illinois 61701 (800-727-5507 or 309-827-5455; fax 888-340-5507 or 309-829-8621) for $89.00 plus shipping and handling.

What Can You Do About Violence? (Session 4): From the series, Questions of Faith for Youth II. The series can be purchased from EcuFilm, 810 Twelfth Avenue South, Nashville, Tennessee 37203, telephone 800-251-4091, for $50.00 plus postage and handling.

Gangs: Turning the Corner (Session 10): Developed by the California Attorney General's Office in 1994 and narrated by James Earl Jones. A law-enforcement perspective. Ask for the condensed 30–minute training program. The video shows groups and individuals involved in prevention and intervention activities and a discussion of suppression strategies. It can be purchased from Film Ideas, Inc., 3710 Commercial Avenue, Suite 13, Northbrook, Illinois 60062 for $69.00.

Youth Struggling for Survival (Session 10): 30–minute documentary featuring Luis Rodriguez, a former gang member who is helping inner-city Chicago youth, including his own son, as they struggle with issues in their lives. The video can be purchased from Films for the Humanities and Sciences, P.O. Box 2053, Princeton, New Jersey 08543-2053, telephone 800-257-5126, for $89.95 plus postage and handling.

PRE-SESSION

FACILITATOR PREPARATION

Have the chairs in a circle. Unless all those who are expected to participate know each other, have name tags and markers available.

Have three sections of the wall covered with newsprint or other large pieces of paper. Using a large-tipped marker, write each of the first two questions from page xvi of the Introduction in the Participant's Book at the top of a sheet. On the third sheet, write "What do you think is the single most important cause of youth violence?" Tape thin-tipped markers to yarn and hang one or two by each sheet. Make sure the yarn is long enough to reach any section of the paper. If you expect more than twenty-five participants, put up two sets of these graffiti sheets, using a different color of paper for each. You may want to make a poster with the quotation from Merry White that appears in the Introduction in the Participant's Book. Ask someone to be prepared to read the Scripture.

If you are using "Children and Canaries" write it on a poster that you can display at the appropriate time. Include the author's name.

For Interfaith Groups or Groups Not Related to the Church

If you don't consider the passage from Micah appropriate, spend more time reflecting on the story of "Children and Canaries."

SESSION OUTLINE
Introduction (5–15 min.)

☐ Welcome participants individually as they arrive. Unless the participants know each other, ask each person to write the name he or she would like to be called on a name tag and put it on.

☐ Graffiti walls: Invite participants to use the hanging markers to respond to the questions that have been posted. If you have two sets, ask half of the participants to work on each set.

☐ As the participants complete their work on the graffiti sheets, go to the one that asks, "What do you think is the single most important cause of youth violence?" Categorize the responses, putting those that are most similar together. A simple grouping might include categories such as family life, mass media, social injustices, and gangs. Include only categories implicit in participant responses. (If you have fewer than six participants, skip the categorization and just see if any two people gave essentially the same response.)

Objectives
☐ Participants will commit to study youth violence together
☐ Participants will practice using the guidelines for discussion

Scripture
☐ Micah 2:1–5,8–9

Supplies
☐ Newsprint graffiti sheets with the questions from page xvi in the Participant's Book, hanging markers
☐ Bibles
☐ *Optional:* Poster with "Children and Canaries" from page 57 in the Participant's Book
☐ *Optional:* Poster with quote from Merry White, from page xviii in the Participant's Book
☐ Photocopy of the questions for each small group
☐ Newsprint and markers
☐ Group Binder

Opening Discussion (10–30 min.)

☐ Invite participants to sit in the circle. Welcome participants. Comment about how the decision to study youth violence was made.

☐ Say: *Youth violence has multiple causes, but as you entered the room, we asked what each of you thinks is the single most important cause. I have tried to classify your responses in categories.* Read the list of categories. Ask participants to quickly form small groups according to which category their response fits in.

☐ As soon as participants are ready, tell them how many minutes you will give them for discussing why they selected a response in that category and select a spokesperson to defend their viewpoint. After 5 minutes, ask the groups if they are ready. If not, give them 2 more minutes. Invite participants to return to the circle. Ask the spokespersons to take turns briefly explaining reasons for the selection of the category they chose.

☐ Say: *Youth violence has many causes, which makes it a challenging topic. Each of us comes to this study with our own presuppositions, motivations, and experiences. It is important that we value the viewpoint of each person as we work together on this issue. In order to make that possible, the Participant's Book provides guidelines for discussion.*

Guidelines (15–25 min.)

☐ Suggest that participants turn to the Guidelines for Dialogue, on page xxi in the Participant's Book. State: *I would like someone to read the first guideline and someone else to read the second, and so on. Who is willing to start?* If there is too much delay at some point, read one yourself, or say, "Who is ready to read?" (If you have worked with this group before and know that all the participants are good readers, you could go around the circle, but if you don't know everyone well, it is best not to do this, as you may end up embarrassing someone.) Ask if anyone has questions about or objections to any of the guidelines.

☐ State: *We will try out the guidelines as we talk together about a couple of the questions from the graffiti sheets. Who would like to share a reason for interest in this topic?* Give everyone who wishes to do so an opportunity to respond. Facilitators may express their reasons.

☐ Then ask: *What are some of the **feelings** you bring to this study? Who would like to share?* If participants are reluctant, say something like this: *Some of us may not want to share our feelings at this time. It is important* *that we be aware that this topic can cause strong feelings. It is all right to share feelings in this group and important that they be respected.*

☐ Ask: *Beyond the personal statements which we have already shared, what are some reasons for taking an interest in youth violence? Why is it important that we do so?* List responses on newsprint or a chalkboard. Suggest to participants that when they read the Introduction at home they might compare the reasons given in the book with those listed by the group.

☐ You may want to ask: *Why should communities of faith be involved in this issue?* List responses on newsprint. You may add ideas from the Introduction in the Participant's Book or suggest that participants look for additional ideas in the Introduction when they read it.

Break (10 min.)
(For 2¹/₂–hour sessions)

Bible Study (15–30 min.)
☐ Summarize the following introductory information: Micah was a prophet in Judah, approximately between 742 and 687 B.C.E. It was a time of political intrigue and economic centralization in Judah and of international conflict. Judah was caught between powerful neighbors, Egypt and Assyria. During much of this time Judah was ruled as an Assyrian satellite and paid heavy taxes to Assyria. Judah was forced to worship Assyrian gods. Micah was concerned with the oppression of the poor (especially peasants) by the wealthy and with the priests who were more interested in getting rich than in rebuking injustice. We will read a couple of short passages in order to understand how Micah saw the situation.

☐ Ask the person who prepared the Scripture reading to read Micah 2:1–5,8–9 aloud now.

☐ Divide into groups of about five persons each, making sure that each group has at least two Bibles to share. Give each group a list of the discussion questions below. Ask them to write their responses to the third question on newsprint. (If you have only one hour, select fewer questions.)

1. Micah suggests that people lie in bed thinking up wicked schemes to put into practice in the morning. What are some of the actions that Micah denounces?

2. One result of this evil is that they take the glory of God from the children. What do you think that might mean?

3. Do you think those who harm young people do it unintentionally, or are they unaware of the damage they do?

4. If Micah were living in this country today, what might he list as evidence that the glory of God is being taken from our children?

☐ Return to the larger group and share lists on newsprint.

"Children and Canaries" (12–30 min., optional)

☐ Display the quotation from James Garbarino, "Children and Canaries." Ask someone to read it aloud.

☐ Divide participants into triads (groups of three). Suggest that participants meet with other people that they do not know very well. Say: *You will have 10 minutes to discuss these questions: How do you respond to this quotation? What feelings does it elicit in you? Be sure each member of your group has a chance to talk.* (If you have omitted the Bible study, ask each group to list on newsprint examples that illustrate the quotation.)

☐ Have the triads return to the larger group and share their lists. Ask: *Who has something you would like to share with the group?*

Intergenerational Study (10–30 min.)

(Omit if you do not have both adults and youth in the group)

☐ If you made a poster with the quotation from Merry White, display it now. Otherwise, ask participants to turn to page xviii in the Participant's Book. Discuss what the quotation means. (If you have both youth and adults in the group, ask youth if they think the statement is true or not, and why. Then ask the adults.)

☐ Ask the youth, then the adults, if the discussion during this session has been carried on in such a way as to increase or narrow the gap between generations. If some participants feel that the discussion thus far has served to increase the gap, ask them to explain. Ask if others feel the same way, and what can be done. (If this discussion is "touchy," remind the group of the discussion guidelines. It is important to work out intergenerational dynamics if group members are to benefit from discussing these issues jointly.)

☐ Ask youth what they need from the adults and ask adults what they need from the youth. (If the group is large, have the youth and adults discuss that question separately, then come together to negotiate.)

Looking Ahead (10 min.)

(Omit if the meeting schedule has been finalized)

☐ If the meeting times for the remainder of the study have not been set, you may want to give several options when the facilitators are available and let the group choose. You may want to negotiate meeting places as well. (If you are meeting at two or three different locations during the remainder of the study, it will be easier to keep track of the schedule if you meet for three or four sessions at one place, then go to the next location for three or four sessions, and so on.)

Action Plan (5–10 min.)

☐ Introduce the idea of Action Plans by summarizing what is said about them in the Introduction in the Participant's Book.

☐ Suggest that participants turn to the end of Session 1 in the Participant's Book. Ask if any participants are ready to commit to the study and would be willing to work on one or more of the options before the next session.

Closing (3–5 min.)

☐ Invite participants to return for Session 1.

☐ Close with prayer, if you wish.

SESSION 1

Do You See That Young Person? Children and Youth at Risk— Children and Youth of Promise

FACILITATOR PREPARATION

Before reading further, write down the first five or ten things that come to mind when you hear the phrase "at-risk youth." Be honest! Don't censor your own thinking. If you are cofacilitating, discuss this and the next step together.

Read the material in the Participant's Book, answering the questions as you go along. Spend some time reflecting on the discussion questions. Decide which ideas you want to mention during the Bible study. If you will use "Elias's Poem" in the session, recruit a reader who will practice reading. Put the chairs in a circle.

For Interfaith Groups or Groups Not Related to the Church

If you do not use the biblical story from the Gospel of Luke, you may spend more time reflecting on "Elias's Poem" or another story that serves the same function.

SESSION OUTLINE
Check-in (10–20 min.)

☐ Welcome participants. Go around the circle so that participants can say their names, the organizations they are with (if your group represents several congregations or other organizations), and—briefly—their main reasons for being interested in youth violence. Facilitators should begin this sharing, modeling brevity in response to the third question.

☐ Ask participants to turn to the Guidelines for Dialogue on page xxi in the Participant's Book. Ask a volunteer to read the first guideline aloud. Have someone else read the second guideline, and so on, until all of them are read. Let participants interrupt if they have questions. (Unless you know everyone in the group well and are confident of their reading ability, it is best not to go around the circle, expecting everyone to read in turn.)

☐ When all of the guidelines have been read, ask *Are there any guidelines you are not sure you understand?* When it appears that everyone understands all the guidelines, ask if everyone is willing to accept the guidelines. If not, negotiate guidelines everyone can accept.

Objectives
☐ Participants will discuss both their own current views and cultural stereotypes of violent youth
☐ Participants will agree to begin gathering data on youth, youth violence, and gangs in their own community

Scripture
☐ Luke 7:36–50

Supplies Needed
☐ Group Binder
☐ Participant's Books
☐ Pencils
☐ Small pieces of paper
☐ Newsprint and markers
☐ Bibles

Off-the-Cuff Thinking (20–35 min., optional)

☐ Make sure each participant has paper and a pen or pencil. Ask participants to write the first ideas that come to mind upon hearing the phrase "at-risk youth" if they did not already do so while reading Session 1 in the Participant's Book. Ask participants to let their ideas flow uncensored and to write whatever comes to mind, whether or not they are true or accurate.

☐ Form groups of three or four persons. Direct participants to share and compare their lists with the group. Each group should form a composite picture of an at-risk youth, emphasizing the ideas that most group members wrote down, or which were written by only one or two members of the group but to which others gave some assent ("Why didn't I think of that?"). A group's "picture" may take the form of a poster-size picture on newsprint, a skit, a "help-wanted" ad, or another creative form.

☐ Ask groups to share skits or post their "pictures" on the wall.

Bible Study (20–30 min.)

[If there are more than twelve persons in your group, divide into small groups; otherwise do this step together. Groups with 2¹/₂-hour sessions may write a parallel story or paraphrase in which the "party crasher" is a teenager with a reputation for violence.]

☐ Read Luke 7:36–50 and discuss the following questions:

  1. It was obvious that Simon saw the woman. From his perspective, she had intruded on his space, spoiled his party, and made a scene. What did Jesus mean when he asked, "Do you see this woman?"

  2. If we hear Jesus asking us, "Do you see this at-risk young person?" what might Jesus want us to see?

  3. If you see a group of young people coming down the street, how do you react toward them? Do you react differently if the members of the group are from a different ethnic group than you are?

  4. Where is the good news for us in this story? Where is the challenge for us?

☐ Return to the circle and ask participants to share insights from their discussion. If groups wrote parallel stories or paraphrases, provide an opportunity for them to be read, and for comments.

Elias's Poem (10–20 min., optional)

☐ Ask the person selected in advance to read "Elias's Poem," which appears on page 3 in the Participant's Book.

☐ After the poem has been read, ask participants to turn to page 4 in their books and look at the reflection questions based on the poem. If you have time, discuss all the questions; if not, select questions on which to focus. If your group includes more than six or eight participants, this discussion should be done in small groups.

Break (10 min.)
(For 2¹/₂–hour sessions)

Approaches to Youth Violence (15–25 min.)
[If you do not have enough time to go through this process, it is important that you take a few minutes to look at Resource 2 together. Ask participants who read the resource before coming to summarize sections. Suggest that participants refer to this resource regularly during the study, and keep the four options for action in mind.]

☐ Ask participants to turn to Resource 2 on page 10 in the Participant's Book. Divide into four groups, and ask each group to read and discuss one of the first four sections of the Resource (Healing of Violence, Prevention, Intervention, and Public Advocacy).

☐ Give each group these instructions: *On newsprint write the name of the approach and a one or two sentence definition of it. Brainstorm some additional ideas that could have been included in the resource. Prepare a brief summary of the approach for the whole group.*

☐ Reassemble the larger group and ask for reports and general comments.

Action Plan (10–22 min.)
☐ Explain the concept of the Action Plan. Action Plans will provide ways for the group to find out and become involved in what is happening in their communities. Action Plans will also give the group access to up-to-date information on youth violence. Ask participants to turn to the Session 1 Action Plan options on page 6 in the Participant's Book. Give them a few moments to look over the options.

☐ Ask for volunteers who are willing to work together before the next session to brainstorm questions the group will want answers for and to discover sources of information in the local community (Option 1).

☐ Ask for volunteers who will "surf the Net" for information. Perhaps some young people in the group who are adept at using computers could meet with adults who would like to learn.

☐ See if anyone is willing to obtain and begin reading one of the books listed in the Action Plan.

Closing (5–8 min.)
☐ Introduce the concept of the Group Binder to the group. Tell the group

that the binder will be used to keep records of their work together. Invite them to bring news clippings and reports from Action Plans to the group for inclusion in the binder.

☐ Ask participants to read the Introduction and Sessions 1 and 2 before the next session and to do the exercises in those sessions.

☐ Read or paraphrase the following: Sometimes some adults see teenagers or children primarily as problems. Sometimes, labels such as "at-risk" are attached to individuals or whole groups of persons. Then it is hard for others to see beyond the label. Howard Thurman, first dean of the Andrew Rankin Memorial Chapel of Howard University, has written that we need to see beyond the plight, predicament, or momentary need of an individual to "something total which must include an awareness of the person's potential. What we need to do is to meet persons where they are and deal with them as if they were where they should be.... Those who love," he says, "always see more than is in evidence at any moment of viewing."[1] Perhaps that is what the Bible story and poem are calling us to do.

☐ If you have plenty of time, stop at the end of the quotation from Thurman, and ask, "If we take Thurman's ideas seriously, how would it change how we see young people who have been labeled as "at-risk?"

☐ Optional: Close with the prayer litany found in Appendix A of the Participant's Book.

Note

1. *In* For the Inward Journey: The Writings of Howard Thurman, *selected by Anne Spencer Thurman (San Diego: Harcourt Brace Jovanovich, 1984), 191-92.*

SESSION 2

WHAT DO CHILDREN AND YOUTH NEED?

FACILITATOR PREPARATION

Before reading further, read the Participant's Book and do the exercises there. Discuss your responses with your cofacilitator(s). Study the Scripture together.

Even if you do not have youth participating in the whole study, invite several teenagers to attend and participate in this session so that adults can hear their perspectives. If you are unable to recruit young people, obtain and preview the video *Warning Signs: A Look At Teenage Violence.* (See Ordering Information on page xvi in the Introduction of this volume.)

Using newsprint or poster board, make posters with the following quotations. On separate pieces of paper, which can be added to the posters at the appropriate times, write the names of those who are quoted and the dates.

"There is no hope for the future of our people if they are dependent on the frivolous youth of today, for certainly all youth are reckless beyond words.... When I was young, we were taught to be discreet and respectful of elders, but the present youth are exceedingly wise and impatient of restraint." (Hesiod, around 800 B.C.E.)

"The children now love luxury; they show disrespect for elders and love chatter in place of exercise. Children are tyrants…. They no longer rise when their elders enter the room. They contradict their parents … and tyrannize their teachers." (Socrates, around 400 B.C.E.)

"The young people of today think of nothing but themselves. They have no reverence for parents or old age. They are impatient of all restraint. They talk as if they alone know everything and what passes for wisdom in us is foolishness in them. As for the girls, they are foolish and immodest and unwomanly in speech, behavior and dress." (Peter the Hermit, around 1083 C.E.)

Write the reflection questions from the Bible study on newsprint. Make a photocopy of the instructions for each small group so that participants can refer to them as they work together. Be sure to have the supplies listed.

For Interfaith Groups or Groups Not Related to the Church

If you do not to use the biblical reflection, spend more time reflecting on the exercises in the Participant's Book. Add the following questions to the fishbowl activity:

1. In what ways are children and youth ignored or neglected in our community or nation?
2. In what ways are children or youth abused in our community or nation?
3. What socially accepted adult behaviors are neglectful or abusive to children and youth in general or to individual children and youth? What impact do you think these behaviors have on young people?

SESSION OUTLINE
Check-in (15–25 min.)

☐ If any new people have joined the study since Session 1, have members who are already participating introduce themselves and give the new participants an opportunity to give their names and state very briefly why they came.

Objectives
☐ Adult participants will listen to young people; youth participants will listen to adults
☐ All participants will discuss the needs of children and youth and how those needs can be met

Scripture
Luke 2:39–52

Supplies Needed
☐ Group Binder
☐ One copy of the directions for small groups
☐ Newsprint and markers
☐ One table for each group making a montage
☐ Collection of recent magazines which could be cut, including news magazines, *Ebony, Emerge, Essence,* sports magazines, women's magazines, and teen magazines, if you are doing the exercise for which they are needed
☐ One posterboard or newsprint for each group that will make montages
☐ Scissors and paste or glue, if you are doing the exercise for which they are needed
☐ Bible study questions on newsprint
☐ Bibles

☐ Ask each participant to pair off with someone he or she does not know well. Give the pairs 2 minutes per person to share what they learned through participating in the Action Plan from Session 1 or anything they thought about since the last session about youth or youth violence.

☐ Come together in the large group again. Ask if anyone has something to share.

"What about These Kids?" (5–10 min., optional)
☐ Put the posters with the quotations by Hesiod, Socrates, and Peter the Hermit on the wall. Have each quotation read, then ask *What sounds familiar about this quotation?*

☐ Post the author's name and the date under each poster. Ask for comments (if time permits).

What's It Like Being a Teen? (20–50 min., optional)
☐ State: *During this session we are going to focus on some of the needs of children and youth. This will be an important grounding for all our work together.*

☐ Ask participants to turn to pages 20–21 in the Participant's Book. Ask if everyone has completed the appropriate exercise. If so, move directly to small groups. (If you have several new participants, or if most of the group members have not completed the exercise, take 6 to 8 minutes to do the exercise. If the majority *have* completed the exercise, you may wish to have them begin the next step; those who need time to finish the exercise may form separate groups when ready.)

 □ If you have invited youth for this session only, skip this exercise and move directly to the fishbowl exercise.

 □ If some members of your group are uncomfortable writing or reading, divide the participants into two groups, one of youth and one of adults. Ask one member of each group to read the questions aloud and give participants about thirty seconds to ponder each one silently.

☐ For the 2½-hour session: Divide into small groups of about six persons each, with teenagers in separate groups from adults. Give the following instructions: *Discuss with your group what it was like to complete the statements in the exercise and what you learned from doing so. You will have about 6 minutes, so make your comments brief and to the point, so everyone will have a chance to speak.*

For the 1-hour session: Ask for comments; then go on to the fishbowl or video. For longer sessions:

☐ After 6 minutes, give these instructions to each group of teens:

 □ Brainstorm together—and list on newsprint—ways in which many adults do not understand teens and their needs.

 □ Look through the magazines and newspapers provided. Cut out pictures that represent ways that the world today is different than when most of the adults in the room grew up.

 □ Make a montage by pasting the pictures on poster board. If you can't find pictures to express all of your ideas, feel free to cut out words (or letters) to include, or express additional ideas with pens or markers.

☐ Hand each group of adults these instructions:

 □ Brainstorm a list of the needs of youth today, and write them on newsprint.

 □ Devise a skit in which teens discuss their needs with one another or with more adults. Be as realistic as you can. Consider using humor, as long as it is in good taste and does not put young people down. Prepare to share the skit with the total group. (If you have no teenagers in the group but have enough adults to have several small groups, give the instructions for teenage groups to one or more of the groups of adults.)

☐ Reassemble into one group. Have each small group share its skit or montage. At the end of each presentation, ask for comments or reflections from other participants.

Fishbowl (30–45 min.)

[If you are unable to have youth participate in this session, skip to the Video Alternative option below.]

☐ Put the chairs in two concentric circles and ask the youth to sit in the middle circle.

☐ Explain that they have formed "a fishbowl." Using the fishbowl approach, only those in the fishbowl—i.e., those in the inner circle—can speak. The role of those in the outer circle (or circles) is to listen.

☐ State: *First, we are going to ask the youth in the fishbowl to comment on the presentation by the adults. How well did the adults express some of the differences between being teens when they were young and what it is like for you being a teenager today? What other differences are you aware of that weren't mentioned?*

☐ Give the youth time to process these questions. Then ask: *What would you like to tell adults about the needs of young people today? What are some ways in which adults show respect to you as a young person? In what ways do you feel disrespected by many adults?*

☐ State: *Now those who are outside the fishbowl (the adults) can have an opportunity to comment on or ask questions about what they have heard. What questions or comments do you have?*

☐ Let the individual to whom the questions are addressed respond. If the discussion gets "hot" remind the group of the guidelines for discussion. If you sense that someone is not feeling heard, reorganize the group and let the person who wants a hearing go into the fishbowl.

☐ Rearrange chairs so everyone is in one circle. Ask: *Did you learn any additional information relevant to the questions we have been discussing during your interview(s) since the last session?* Have participants turn to Resource 3 in the Participant's Book and skim the headings to see if there are ideas in the handout not discussed thus far. If so, ask someone to read through the relevant section and ask for comments on it.

Video Alternative (30–45 min.)

☐ In lieu of having youth participate in this session, show the 23–minute video *Warning Signs: A Look at Teenage Violence*.

☐ Ask participants to discuss as many of the following questions as time allows:

1. What are some underlying causes why these young people became involved in violence? Where did they experience violence or see it modeled?
2. The video says that young people need someone to pay attention to them. What does that mean? In what ways did you need or receive attention when you were young?
3. How can adults help young people like these realize that they have other choices?
4. What can we do to create a safe environment for young people?
5. How can we help young people feel that they are accepted and important to the community?

☐ If you have time, ask someone to role-play being one of the young people in the video (or someone in a similar situation) before they became involved in violence. Ask one or two others to role-play adults, such as teachers or other youth with whom they might interact. Discuss whether or not the actions taken in the role play would be helpful to the youth.

Break (10 min.)
(For 2¹/₂-hour sessions)

Bible Study (10–20 min.)
☐ Ask for a volunteer who will read Luke 2:39–52 when asked.
☐ Post the following questions and suggest that each person listen with them in mind:

1. Before and after the story of the boy Jesus in the temple, Luke tells us how Jesus grew. Why do you think this idea is repeated?
2. What do we learn about Jesus' environment that might help us understand how he grew?
3. What needs of young people are reflected in this story?
4. To what extent did Jesus' parents understand his needs?
5. The reflections in the Participant's Book suggest that any child or teenager who is taken seriously might astonish adults with his or her wisdom. How do you respond to that idea?
6. What are some ways in which adults can show children and teenagers that they value them as persons, value their ideas, and take them seriously?

☐ Discuss the questions listed above with the whole group or in small groups. You may draw on the following reflections to enrich the discussion if you wish.

Further Reflections on Luke 2:39–52

(For facilitator use as desired)

At the end of the celebration, as Jesus' family began the journey back home, they assumed that Jesus was with friends. At twelve, Jesus would have been considered a young man, not a small child needing close watching. Mary and Joseph were part of a culture that would have agreed with the African proverb that it takes a whole village to raise a child. Neighborhood children or youth would congregate, and the nearest adults would keep an eye on them. Consequently, Mary and Joseph had gone a whole day's journey before they discovered that their son was not with the other boys. This is not really a story about a lost boy, however, but about a boy who knew—or at least was beginning to understand—God's call on his life.

When Mary and Joseph found Jesus, he was situated as a student—listening to the rabbis, asking them questions, answering their questions. They were "struck by" his responses to their questions. Luke tells the story in a calm, restrained manner, in contrast to an extrabiblical account that says Jesus was instructing the rabbis and priests about a multitude of subjects, including medicine and astronomy.

Some people see this story in Luke as evidence of the divinity of Jesus. It seems to me, however, that it shows a very human side of Jesus as an adolescent. He was a young person with good ideas, with an ability to think and to communicate. The more we listen carefully to and dialogue deeply with children and adolescents, the more we will be struck by their ideas.

Some people may be offended by the comment in the Participant's Book that Mary made a common parenting error, but Mary was human. Still, despite seeming to take personally what Jesus did, she didn't overreact by using physical punishment, yelling, or lecturing!

Action Plan (5–15 min.)

☐ Ask for volunteers who will conduct an interview or visit an agency or program working with youth and make a report, alone or in pairs. This option is a good opportunity for a young person and an adult to work together.

☐ Ask for volunteers who would like to "surf the Net." If most participants want to do the Internet Option, suggest taking turns. If you have several new members, repeat the idea that some young people in the group who are adept at using computers could meet with some adults who would like to learn and do this assignment together. Distribute the web addresses and assignments.

☐ Ask if anyone else is willing to read one of the books listed at the end of Session 1.

Closing (5 min., optional)

☐ If you would like, sing a song such as "Never Too Late," by Mona Bagasao,[1] "Faces of the Children," by Sr. Kathy Sherman,[2] or "Drops of Water," by Jim Strathdee.[3]

☐ You may wish to have someone read the quotation in Resource 1 and sit in silence for a few moments reflecting on it.

☐ Close with prayer if you wish.

Notes

1. *From* Take a Stand! Songs to Make a Better World *(Carlsbad, Calif.: Better World Artists and Activists Guild and the American Baptist Board of Education and Publication, 1996), 34–35. Book and CD for $14.95 plus postage and handling 800-ABC-3USA, ext. 2260; or 800-236-9751; or contact the Better World Artists and Activists Guild by e-mail at jlbwaag@sol.com.*

2. *Available for purchase from the Sisters of St. Joseph of LaGrange, 1515 West Ogden Avenue, LaGrange Park, Illinois 60525-1721; 708-354-9573; fax 708-354-9573.*

3. *In Ruth C. Duck & Michael G. Bausch, eds.,* Everflowing Streams *(New York: Pilgrim Press, 1981), 60.*

SESSION 3

A Place to Belong?
Joining Gangs/Going It Alone

Facilitator Preparation

Before reading further, answer for yourself the questions you will pose to the group in this session. Discuss your responses with your cofacilitator(s). Study the Scripture passage together.

Recruit actors or readers to present the playlet "Tamar's Ruse." Ask them to prepare ahead of time. The script can be found in Appendix B on page 142 in the Participant's Book.

Make photocopies of the directions for brainstorming groups. If your total group is large, plan to subdivide into groups of five or six for this exercise. Half of the small groups will need instructions for Group A and the other half for Group B. It will help facilitate the process if you have already put the headings on newsprint for Groups A and B.

Be sure to have the supplies listed. Set up the table(s) for making montages, and have the poster board, magazines, scissors, and paste or glue set out on the table(s) ready for use.

If you plan to use the poem, "Neighborhood Gangs vs. Neighborhood Schools and Churches" in the closing, find a good reader who will practice ahead of time. The author, James McGrew, is a performer who identifies himself as a social poet. This poem should be read rhythmically, like a rap song.

For Interfaith Groups or Groups Not Related to the Church

Since this biblical passage is from the Hebrew Scripture, it is part of the heritage of both Christian and Jewish groups. If this passage is not appropriate for your context, substitute a story that is, but that will serve as a background for raising the same issues. Or spend more time reflecting on the poem by James McGrew.

SESSION OUTLINE
Check-in (15–25 min.)

☐ Ask participants to pair off with someone they haven't paired up with yet and share highlights of what they learned through the Action Plan or share something they have been thinking of since the last session. Each participant will have 2 minutes, during which he or she should not be interrupted. When 2 minutes are up, ask the second person in each pair to share.

☐ Have everyone return to the large circle. Take 8 to 10 minutes to give those who want to share something an opportunity to do so. Make sure that no one dominates the time, so anyone who really wants to share can do so. Provide opportunities for others to respond to what they hear.

☐ Ask everyone to turn in the written reports of interviews. These can be duplicated for everyone in the group and put in the Group Binder.

Objectives
☐ Participants will discuss reasons young people join gangs or become loners
☐ Participants will list positive benefits which gangs may provide their members
☐ Participants will agree to interview young people concerning the benefits they perceive from group memberships

Scripture
☐ Genesis 38

Supplies Needed
☐ Newsprint prepared for the Input section
☐ Newsprint and markers
☐ Photocopies of the brainstorming instructions for Groups A and B
☐ Bibles

Bible Study (20–30 min.)

[Note: You may draw on the reflections on Genesis 38 (at the end of this chapter) to enrich the discussion or answer questions.]

☐ Introduce the skit briefly, by saying *We will begin with a playlet based on Genesis 38, entitled "Tamar's Ruse."* Ask those who have prepared to act out or read the play to do so.

☐ If you have ten or more participants, divide into groups of five or six to discuss the play. Give each group the following questions. (If you are running behind schedule or have only a short session, omit questions 1 and 4.)

1. What did you find interesting about this story?
2. How do you think Tamar felt when Judah sent her away from his household?
3. In the Bible story, Judah says that Tamar was "more right" (or "more righteous," depending on which translation you are using) than he. Why do you think he says that?
4. When should we put the interests of the community above our own interests? When should we risk our own interests for the welfare of others?
5. How would you define a "meaningful place of belonging"? Where or with whom do you feel a sense of belonging? How does that affect your sense of identity?
6. It is often said that many youth in the U.S. believe there is no safe and meaningful place of belonging for them. How do you respond to that statement?

☐ Call participants back into one circle. Ask *Who would be willing to state one main idea from their small group that they found helpful?* and *How would you define "a meaningful place of belonging"?*

Break (10 min.)
(For 2¹/₂–hour sessions)

Brainstorming (15–40 min.)

☐ Divide into two groups (or if your group is large, into two or more sets of small groups) and label them Group A and Group B. Give each group a written copy of its instructions, its newsprint, and a marker.

Instructions for Group A: Brainstorm reasons why you think youth join groups, whether they are Scouts, Awanas, Pioneer Clubs, or other church youth groups, sports teams, or other groups, and what you think youth gain from such groups. List all the reasons you can think of on newsprint. When you are finished brainstorming, go back and put an asterisk in front of each one that you think may apply to at least some youth gangs.

Instructions for Group B: Brainstorm a list of reasons you think young people join gangs, and the benefits they expect to receive from gang membership, and list responses on newsprint. When you are finished brainstorming, go back and put an asterisk in front of each response which the group thinks could apply also to such groups as Scouts, Awanas, Pioneer Clubs, sports teams, and so on.

☐ Reassemble in one large group. Ask each group to share the results of its work with the larger group. Then compare the results arrived at by the two groups.

☐ Ask: *What have you learned from this exercise?*

☐ Suggest that participants turn to Resource 4, "Why Youth Join Gangs—Some Opinions," on page 39 in the Participant's Book. Ask: Which ideas in this resource were reflected in our discussion?

Action Plan (10–40 min.)

☐ State: *The most important Action Plan for this session involves interviewing persons, including—if possible—some who are or have been involved with gangs. We will get better information if several participants actually interview current and former gang members. We recognize that not all participants will be willing or able to undertake this assignment, so there are other interview categories, also.* Look at the most sensitive categories listed in the suggested Action Plan in the Participant's Book first and see who is willing to try. Look next at the other interview categories and see who is willing to do interviews.

☐ If you have time, brainstorm questions; if not, arrange for other group members to contact the interviewers with their suggestions.

Closing (10–15 min., optional)

☐ Invite participants to meditate silently as someone reads the poem, "Neighborhood Gangs vs. Neighborhood Schools & Churches" from page 36 in the Participant's Book.

☐ Consider singing, "Heart to Heart," from *Take a Stand! 23 Songs to*

Make a Better World (Better World Artists and Activists Guild [BWAAG] and American Baptist Board of Education and Publication, 1996); for information call 800–458–3766.

REFLECTIONS ON GENESIS 38

Biblical scholar Susan Niditch says that in tribal, patriarchal culture the role of the young woman was to bear offspring. A woman was brought into her husband's clan through her children. The idea of levirate marriage (a man marrying or having sex with his brother's widow to provide offspring for his dead brother) was to "avoid a sociological misfit," a woman who belonged neither to her father's house nor to her husband's clan. She says, "The social fabric as a whole is weakened by her problem, and extremely unusual means are allowed to rectify the situation."[1]

In his commentary on Genesis,[2] Walter Brueggemann says that the passage draws "a striking contrast ... between this man who has standing and status in the community and this woman who stands outside the law and is without legal recourse." Brueggemann then refers to Luke 12:48, in which Jesus says, "From everyone to whom much has been given, much will be required; and from the one to whom much has been entrusted, even more will be demanded." Then Brueggemann adds,

> Not much, in fact nothing, has been given to Tamar. And she is not indicted for much.... the narrative not only minimizes her wrong but vindicates her. The story ends without stigma attached to her. By contrast, Judah is the one to whom much as been given: sons, goods, standing. From him, more is asked.... To be sure, a kind of risk is asked of Judah.... What is asked of him is that he risk his son, even his last son, available for the solidarity and future of the community now focused in the person of this defenseless widow. The offense of Judah.... is the sin of looking after private interest at the expense of the community.

Brueggemann goes on to say, "Tamar has committed the kind of sin the 'good' people prefer to condemn—engaging in deception and illicit sex and bringing damage to a good family." Judah, on the other hand, "has violated her right to well-being and dignity in the community."

Brueggemann goes on to say that this "interpretation has no desire to glorify Tamar or to make a virtue of her actions." Nevertheless, though she broke the mores—and even the laws—of her society, she is not condemned. She did so in order to make a place for herself, a place in which her needs could be met and she could have some sense of belonging. Underlying the text is a sense that everyone has a right to have a safe and meaningful place, a place of belonging, a place where needs are met. Sin, in this story, is not Tamar's use of her sexuality nor her deception of Judah. Rather it is the action of Judah in excluding her from a meaningful place in society and the system that allows her to be excluded.

Indeed, had Judah chosen to deny the truth of her statement linking him with her pregnancy, she doubtless would have been executed. Her word would not have stood against his, because he had high status in society. Any society that excludes people from safe and meaningful places of belonging is unjust and needs to be changed.

Tamar was "more righteous" than Judah because she used her few resources to overcome injustice, while he refused justice to her. Judah became "righteous" when, instead of getting defensive or denying his role, he recognized what he had done and acknowledged Tamar's humanity and right to a meaningful life.

Notes

1. Susan Niditch, "The Wronged Woman Righted: An Analysis of Genesis 38," Harvard Theological Review, 72:143–149.
2. Walter Brueggemann, "Genesis," Interpretation: A Bible Commentary for Teaching and Preaching (Atlanta: John Knox Press, 1982). The following discussion draws from pages 309–311.

SESSION 4

WHAT SHALL WE DO WITH OUR FEAR?

FACILITATOR PREPARATION

Read the Scripture passage for this session. Spend some time reflecting on the discussion questions. Read the material in the Participant's Book.

If you are using the recommended video, watch it in advance, and discuss the questions about it with your cofacilitators. Also, if you are using the video, you might want to put up a display of articles about violence in your local community. If you have only one hour, you may have to decide whether to use the video or clipping activity or to discuss the story of the aging apostle, so as to leave time for the Action Plan.

If you wish, ask participants to prepare the Scripture reading in advance.

For Interfaith Groups or Groups Not Related to the Church

If you do not use the Scripture or the story of the apostle John, substitute another story suitable for the group or spend more time discussing the video and/or reflecting on the story of Ross Misher.

SESSION OUTLINE
Check-in (10–25 min.)

☐ Ask participants to pair off with someone they haven't paired off with very often, and share highlights of what they learned through the Action Plan or something they have been thinking about since the last session. When 2 minutes have elapsed, say: *Half your time is up; if only one of you has been sharing, it is time to let your partner talk.*

☐ Have everyone return to the large circle. Ask: *Who has something they would like to share?* After someone shares, you may ask, *Would anyone like to respond?* (If you have a 2½–hour session, you will have time to encourage in-depth sharing.)

Violence and Fear (25–45 min.)

☐ **Option 1:** Show the 17–minute video, *What Can You Do About Violence?*, from the series, Questions of Faith for Youth II.

Option 2: Divide into groups of five or six persons. Give each group a pile of recent newspapers and news magazines. IMPORTANT: At least some of the newspapers should be local papers. Give the groups 10 to 15 minutes to find and clip out articles dealing with violence in the U.S., including your own community.

Objectives
☐ Participants will discuss the kinds of violence they have experienced
☐ Participants will discuss fear of violence, and how to overcome fear

Scripture
☐ 1 John 4:7–12,18–21

Supplies Needed
☐ Group Binder
☐ Timer
☐ *What Can You Do about Violence?* video or a collection of recent (local) newspapers and news magazines
☐ Newsprint and markers (or chalkboard and chalk)
☐ Bibles

☐ Ask participants to form pairs. Instruct pairs that each partner will be given an opportunity to express his or her reaction to the video (or news clippings) without interruption. While it is one person's turn to talk, the other is to listen only. When the timer goes off, the other person will respond to the video or news clippings without interruption. This will give each person the opportunity to process his or her own thoughts. The listener is to listen with appreciation but not validate or argue with the other person's view. Ask each pair to decide who will speak first. Set the timer for 1½ minutes and ask the first person to begin; when time is up, ask the first speaker to finish his or her sentence. Set the timer for 1½ minutes for the second person.

☐ Have participants bring their chairs into one big circle. Discuss the following questions. (If you have a shorter session, select the more personal questions, such as questions 1, 2, 5, and 7.)

1. To what did you respond most strongly while watching the video (or cutting and reading the news articles)?
2. What experiences have you had with violence?
3. What kinds of violence exist in your neighborhood or community?
4. What are some causes of violence identified in the video? What additional causes are you aware of?
5. Are you afraid of violence? How do you handle that fear?
6. It has been said that young people often feel powerless in the face of violence. Do you think that is true? If so, what are some sources of this feeling of powerlessness?
7. People feel less powerless when they are doing something to deal with issues. What can young people—and others—do about the issue of violence? What can *you* do?

Break (10 min.)
(For 2½-hour sessions)

Bible Study (6–20 min.)
The Bible study can be done in small groups if you prefer. In that case, you may want to ask the small groups to share some of their discussion with the larger group when you reassemble.

☐ Have participants open their Bibles to 1 John 4. Ask for a volunteer to read verses 7–12 and another to read verses 19–21.

☐ Say: *Express some of the key ideas in this passage in your own words.* Write the group's responses on newsprint or chalkboard, if you wish. Record them in the Group Binder for future reference.

☐ Say: *Many of our fears in relation to the issue of violence are normal and natural. How can we support one another so as to overcome these fears and be free to do what God calls us to do?* Write these on the newsprint as well, and again, record them in the Group Binder so you can refer to them from time to time.

☐ Read (or ask someone else to read) the story "The Aging Apostle and the Gang Member," on page 46 in the Participant's Book. Ask participants how they see this story in relation to the Scripture text. If time permits, ask several of the reflection questions that follow the story.

Action Plan (10–40 min.)

☐ Refer to the lists of persons suggested for interviews in Sessions 1 and 2. Ask if the interviews that were done suggested ideas for other possible interview subjects. Then ask for volunteers to do an interview before the next session.

☐ Ask if any participants drafted goals and steps using Resource 4. Into which approach or approaches to youth violence listed in Resource 2 do their draft plans fall? After drafts are shared, ask *Which plans are most similar? Which seem to have the most possibility for our group? Are we ready to pick one of these plans and ask two or three people to help the person who wrote it to refine it?* If the group answers yes to the last question, select a small group of participants willing to work together on refining the plan, and ask them to bring it back to the next session for further consideration. (If your group is composed of fewer than eight individuals, you may do this step together during your session time.)

At this stage, you may wish to work on a "small" plan as a way of getting involved more directly in the issue of youth violence, rather than on a full-fledged plan. However, whenever the group is ready, you may choose to use the planning process spelled out in Resource 5. Different kinds of congregations and groups find different planning processes more productive, so feel free to use an alternative process if that suits your group better.

Closing (5–10 min.)

☐ Ask if participants would like to make a commitment to be mutually supportive as the group continues to explore and become involved in the issue of youth violence. Ask what commitments participants are willing to make.

☐ You may wish to close with this prayer by Margaret Anne Huffman:

O God, not only is our world violent, *we* are violent. We bait
the trap of evil ourselves when we make wrong choices. No

wonder you keep reminding us to choose life; you know our tendencies! Sometimes acting alone and sometimes acting together, we hurt others. Hear our confession for mild and brutal deeds, for passive and aggressive acts of ...

... cynicism and apathy, quiet forms of violence;

... lukewarm concern when we could care as passionately as you do;

... violent thought (if thoughts are deeds, then we've maimed many);

... not speaking up when we hear crude, bigoted, or inflammatory remarks, jokes;

... willfully misunderstanding others' points of view;

... holding grudges and withholding true forgiveness;

... lashing out in spite and sarcasm;

... making gestures, rude faces to imitate others, especially kids;

... yelling, hitting, slapping, and trying to justify ourselves (we have no excuse);

... ignoring signs of family or child abuse and not getting involved;

... not being Good Samaritans for fear of getting hurt ourselves, and so letting someone suffer, even die, doubly betrayed, as we passed by.

We fall so far short of who we can be. We fail in small ways, even if not in big ways. Forgive us, God of mercy, when our deeds do not match our words about peace and love. Help us to bring word and deed together like hands in prayer, two halves of a whole, forgiven and renewed persons. Amen.[1]

Note

1. Margaret Ann Huffman, "We Are Them: A Confession." In "Through the Valley ..." Prayers for Violent Times (Valley Forge, Pa.: Judson Press, 1996), 112. Reprinted by permission of the publisher.

SESSION 5

A NOXIOUS CULTURE OF VIOLENCE?

FACILITATOR PREPARATION

Read the material for this session in the Participant's Book, responding to questions.

Write the words of Matthew 5:9 in large letters on a poster board or piece of newsprint. If you have someone in your group with artistic gifts, you might ask that person to make the poster and to illustrate the verse.

Write out the words of the following quotation from James Garbarino in large letters, banner style, with the four parts, as marked with the slanted lines, on four different pieces of newsprint: "One important element in the social toxicity of American culture lies in our acceptance of violence // as a technique for punishment, // a strategy for dealing with conflict, // and a form of entertainment."[1] Add Garbarino's name to the end of the quotation. When you are ready to use the quotation in the session, you will post the first part of the quote directly in front of the group circle, and the other three parts in order in other parts of the room.

Photocopy Handouts 5A and 5B. Handout 5B should be enlarged and photocopied on card stock if possible. Participants will appreciate a choice of colors, if possible.

Be prepared for the possibility of resistance to material in this session. Individuals who enjoy media violence are likely to resist the idea that it is a toxic element in North American culture. Also, research on the relationship between physical punishment and violence has been largely ignored by both scholars and the popular media. Parents who spank, and many who were spanked as children and do not believe it harmed them, will resist connecting corporal punishment with violence. You may question these connections yourself. Encourage skeptical participants to listen to these viewpoints and withhold judgment at this point. Encourage them to read some of the recommended resources in order to understand the issues better.

Objectives

☐ Participants will be able to state ways they can be peacemakers
☐ Participants will discuss ways North American culture contributes to the problem of youth violence

Scripture

☐ Matthew 5:9,38–45

Supplies Needed

☐ Group Binder
☐ Poster board with the words of Matthew 5:9
☐ Poster with quotation from James Garbarino
☐ Three copies of instructions for small groups for discussion of Garbarino quotation
☐ Pencils and paper
☐ Bibles
☐ Photocopies of Handout 5A for each participant
☐ Photocopies of handout 5B on card stock for each participant (if you are making Peace Cubes)
☐ Thin-tipped markers (if you are making Peace Cubes)

For Interfaith Groups or Groups Not Related to the Church

If you choose not to use the biblical material from Matthew, reflect primarily on "The Forgiveness Story—The Story of a Contemporary Peacemaker."

SESSION OUTLINE
Check-in (15–20 min.)

☐ Ask participants to pair off. If your group is intergenerational, encourage youth to partner with adults. Give pairs 5 minutes to discuss the Action Plan in which they participated, the reading they have done on youth violence, or what they have been thinking about since the previous session. After 2½ minutes, announce that half the time is over, so if one person has been doing most of the talking thus far, it is time to be quiet and listen to the partner. ☐ Form the circle again and ask individuals to share with the whole group.

Violence in the Culture (10–30 min.)
☐ Divide into groups of about six to eight persons. Give each group newsprint and a marker. Give these instructions: *In American English, we use a lot of words with violent referents even when we are not discussing violence, per se. For instance, if someone undercuts me at work, I may say, "He stabbed me in the back." Come up with as many commonly used violent figures of speech and images as you can in 5 minutes. Do not include literal usages, such as if someone actually was stabbed.* As soon as the directions are clear, let the groups begin.
☐ After 5 minutes, gather all the participants together and have them post their lists. Ask one group to call out one of the figures of speech or images they listed. Pick out the key word in the phrase, such as stab, kill, gun, etc. Ask if other groups have listed phrases using a form of that word. If so have those phrases listed next. Then go to another group and ask for a phrase, repeating this process until all the phrases have been listed.
☐ Ask: *What feelings did this exercise elicit in you? What might this list tell us about the culture in which we live?* Distribute Handout 5A for participants to consider other violent metaphors used in our culture.

Peacemakers (10–20 min., optional)
☐ Ask participants individually or in pairs to define the word *peacemaker.*
☐ Ask participants to name some peacemakers they know about. List them on newsprint. Ask those who suggest names to explain briefly why they consider that person to be a peacemaker.
☐ Ask: *What is a peacemaker?* After a definition is volunteered, ask *Who has a very similar definition?* Comment on how many hands are raised.
☐ Then ask *Who has a different definition?* Continue this process until no one has a different definition.
☐ Ask: *What did you learn from someone else's definition that might inspire you to change or expand yours? Do you have any names to add to the list of peacemakers?*

Bible Study (15–20 min.)

☐ Post Matthew 5:9 (near the list of peacemakers if you made one) and read it in unison. Ask a volunteer to read Matthew 5:38–45. Ask: *What light does this Scripture throw on our definitions of peacemaker?*

☐ Divide into groups of three or four people. Give the following instructions: *Read Matthew 5:9,38–45 again. Prepare a paraphrase of the Scripture, putting it into the language of today. Replace the specific commands about turning the other cheek, etc., with examples that have particular meaning today.*

☐ Have each group write its paraphrase on newsprint. (If you don't have enough time to write actual paraphrases, just ask participants to come up with examples of how the specific commands might be interpreted for today.)

☐ Form the circle again and ask groups to share their paraphrases or examples. Ask for comments.

Break (10 min.)
(For 2¹/₂–hour sessions)

Making Peace in a Violent Society (20–35 min.)

☐ Post on the wall the quotation from James Garbarino that you prepared, putting the sections in order around the room. Mention that there may be controversy on the points about to be discussed. Then read or ask someone to read the whole quotation.

☐ Have participants form three groups. Distribute to each group newsprint and markers. Each group will explore one of Garbarino's points concerning our culture's acceptance of violence—as "a technique for punishment," as "a strategy for dealing with conflict," and as "a form of entertainment." Ask participants to take their chairs and form a circle near the part of the quotation they want to discuss. (Note that groups should form under the second, third, and fourth panel, not the first.)

☐ Give each group the following questions. Each group should select a reporter and record the group's responses to the first two questions on newsprint.

    1. Do you agree with Garbarino's assessment that violence is an accepted technique for punishment / a strategy for dealing with conflict / a form of entertainment? (Discuss only the one assigned

to your group.) Why or why not? If you agree, how do you feel about that?

2. What are some ways we can be peacemakers by counteracting this element of violence in our culture?

3. In what ways does this entire quotation from Garbarino challenge you to change your own life?

☐ Re-form the circle and give each small group an opportunity to report. After each report, ask for comments. (If you are having a fruitful discussion and don't want to cut it too short, skip the next section of the session plan.)

Contemporary Peacemaking (10–15 min., optional)

If you are running short on time, the facilitators may choose between the exercises in Option 1 ("The Forgiveness Party—The Story of a Contemporary Peacemaker") and Option 2 ("The Peacemaking Cube"). Alternatively, you may offer participants the choice, or use Option 1 during the session and suggest that participants do Option 2 at home.

☐ **Option 1:** "The Forgiveness Party—The Story of a Contemporary Peacemaker"

▫ Read or tell the story "The Forgiveness Party—The Story of a Contemporary Peacemaker," found on page 60 in the Participant's Book.

▫ Discuss the questions following the story.

☐ **Option 2:** The Peacemaking Cube

▫ Give each participant a copy of Handout 5B on card stock. Distribute scissors and markers as well, at least enough that participants can share easily.

▫ Have participants select six quotes from those found in Resource 6 or from among the boxed quotes in Session 5 in the Participant's Book.

▫ Give the following instructions: *Write one quotation (and the name of the person quoted) on each panel of the handout, using thin-tipped markers. Cut out the outline of the larger shape, and fold along the dotted lines to form a cube.*

▫ Suggest that participants keep the cube on their dining room table and read one side before each meal. If you have extra copies of the handout, participants can also make peacemaking cubes for friends or people in the community who are (or should be) interested in stopping youth violence.

Action Plan (5–25 min.)

☐ Ask if anyone has an update on an ongoing Action Plan activity.

☐ Ask for volunteers to try the Action Plans recommended in Session 5. Note that those contacting the Families Against Violence Advocacy Network (FAVAN) do not have to commit to a specific action at this stage. They will get information on FAVAN and what, if anything, is being done in the local community, and can recommend further action later.

Closing (5 min., optional)

☐ Ask a volunteer to read the Family Pledge of Nonviolence (page 66 in the Participant Book).

☐ Sing together "You Make Strong" or "Peace is the Feeling," from *Take a Stand: 23 Songs to Make a Better World.*[2]

☐ Close in prayer, if you wish.

Notes

1. *James Garbarino,* Raising Children in a Socially Toxic Environment *(San Francisco: Jossey-Bass Publishers, 1995), 68. Reprinted by permission.*

2. Take a Stand: 23 Songs to Make a Better World *(Carlsbad, Calif.: Better World Artists and Activists Guild, and Valley Forge, Pa.: Educational Ministries, American Baptist Churches, USA, 1996), 2829, 3637.*

Some Violent Images in the English Language

(Note: In some cases it is not possible to say whether the image builds on violence against human beings or not.)

We **annihilated** their team.

I'm in the **army** of the Lord, the Prince of Peace.

He is such a **straight arrow**; I don't think you could tempt him to do that.

She is **battling** cancer.

We win the **battle** against violence.

She **blasted me out of the water** with her creative new ideas.

They introduced the new product with an advertising **blitz.**

I was going to take the last piece of pie, but he **beat me to the draw.**

Smart-bomb drugs will know how to go directly to the affected cells.

We sent out a request for suggestions and were **bombarded** with ideas!

He **dropped a bomb** in the meeting by announcing his resignation.

Instead of numbering the points, why not use **bullets**?

He's fast as a **bullet!**

What **caliber** of person is he, anyway?

You knew he wanted your job; why didn't you do something to **cut him off at the pass?**

She is **fighting** depression.

They **fought** the good **fight.**

He **gunned** the engine.

Did you stick to your **guns**?

I can tell he is **gunning** for me.

I wondered about it for a long time. Suddenly **it hit me.**

How many **hits** did the website get today?

He is really nasty in his (verbal) **attacks;** that was **hitting below the belt.**

"**Hit 'em again,** harder, harder!" (school cheer)

Hit the deck!

Hit the ground running!

Don't tell any more of those jokes tonight! You are **killing** me!

We will buy up a million shares, and move in for **the kill** (i.e., take over the company).

If he leaves, **it will kill her** (i.e., she will be very unhappy).

She made **a killing** on the stock market.

He **knifed** her **in the back** (i.e., he betrayed her).

That was a **knife through the heart!**

Knock it off.

That's a **knock** on him (a negative about him).

When Michael Jordan played for them, the Chicago Bulls **massacred** every team in the league!

You want to tell me what happened? OK, **shoot.**

She **shot** that idea down in a hurry.

That was a **shot** in the dark!

We need someone to write a press release; will you take a **shot** at it?

When her son left home, it was a **shot** through the heart.

He hit the accelerator and **shot** forward.

We have to get his attention; let's try **a shot across the bow.**

When I did that, I really **shot myself in the foot!**

I can't get my car started; will you give it a **shot?**

I like candidates who **shoot from the hip.**

You have to give her credit—she's **a straight shooter.**

Let's **shoot** the works.

He **shot** his wad at the mall.

Was it a **shotgun** wedding?

Hey Mom, can I ride **shotgun?**

He's been **sniping** at me all week.

We **slaughtered** the opposition!

It is hard for me now that he is gone, but I'll have to **soldier on.**

"Onward, Christian **soldiers,** marching as to **war** … " (Christian hymn).

I'm not sure if I can make it work, but I'll take a **stab** at it.

I trusted her with my secret, and she **stabbed me in the back.**

You **hit the target** with that idea.

To design a marketing plan, we need to decide what groups to **target.**

He is a real **trooper!**

What thoughts does that **trigger** for you?

To **take action.**

What can we say or do that might **trigger** a response from her?

Do you think the **war on drugs** was more successful than the **war on poverty?**

CUBE PATTERN

Directions: Photocopy this page and cut out the cube. (You can enlarge the image on your photocopier.) Fold along the dotted lines; then unfold it and lay it flat. On each side write one of the "Peace Quotes." If you have time, decorate the sides. Fold the box and glue or tape it shut. Keep it handy and turn it each day. Read the quotation on top, and think about it.

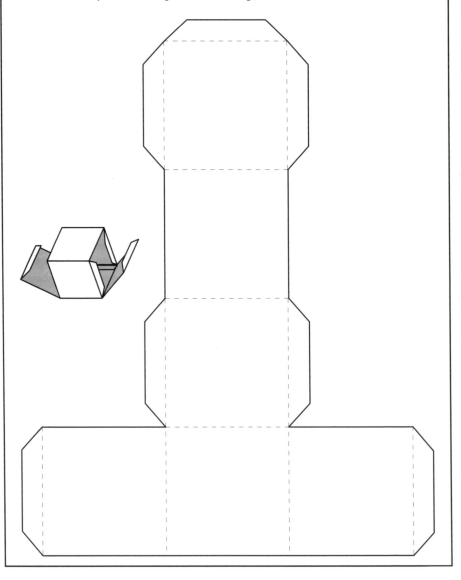

SESSION 6

WHAT'S GOING ON HERE?
ANOMIE, TRAUMA, AND VIOLENCE

FACILITATOR PREPARATION

Begin by reading Session 6 in the Participant's Book. This session has a lot of material that may be new to many people, perhaps even to you. If you are doing one-hour sessions with your group, devote two sessions to this material if at all possible.

Decide ahead of time, on the basis of your knowledge of the group, whether to play balloon volleyball or substitute a less active game. Note that there are two different handouts for the game, each with the same title, "Double-Balloon Volleyball." If you decide to substitute a less active game, be sure to prepare two sets of differing rules so the group has the experience of trying to play together using different rules. Make photocopies of each version of the rules handout for half the members of the group. Stack them, alternating the two versions.

Set the chairs a little farther apart than usual when you set up the room. Prepare for balloon volleyball by deciding where it will be played. If you have a volleyball court or net you can use, that would be best. Otherwise, tape a string between two chairs or two walls.

Decide whether to ask someone else to present a summary of pages 81–83 in the Participant's Book concerning trauma and violence or to do it yourself, or decide if you will have various members of the group read different sections aloud. If you have someone in your community who has expertise on Post-traumatic Stress Disorder (PTSD) or brain development, ask that person to make a presentation and answer participants' questions instead of doing the portion of the session plan on PTSD.

Objectives

☐ Participants will discuss the meaning of *anomie* and its impact on youth
☐ Participants will be able to describe the impact of trauma on children and youth
☐ Participants will be able to explain the interrelationship between *anomie* and trauma and between each of them and violence

Scripture

☐ Nehemiah 5:1–19

Supplies Needed

☐ Group Binder
☐ Newsprint and markers
☐ Coach's whistle
☐ Two or three balloons, inflated firm enough for use in balloon volleyball
☐ Photocopies of each set of rules for balloon volleyball, enough for half the participants to have one and half to have the other
☐ Bibles

For Interfaith Groups or Groups Not Related to the Church

The story of Nehemiah can be handled as a historical incident happening in the ancient Middle East, so it is possible that all partners would be comfortable using it. If not, you may want to focus reflections on the story of Kevin Tucker (see pages 85–86 in the Participant's Book.)

SESSION OUTLINE
Check-in (15–25 min.)

☐ Ask participants to pair off with someone they haven't paired up with yet and share highlights of what they learned through the Action Plan; something they have read, relevant to youth violence; or thoughts they have had since the last session. Each participant will have 2 minutes. When 2 minutes have elapsed, ask the second person in each pair to share.

☐ Have everyone return to the large circle. Take 8 to 10 minutes to give those who want to share something an opportunity to do so. Make sure that no one dominates the time, so anyone who really wants to share can do so.

☐ Ask if anyone has anything to contribute to the Group Binder. Let each say very briefly what it is, and add it to the binder now.

Double–Balloon Volleyball (8–15 min.)

☐ Tell participants that the group is going to play a little game of double-balloon volleyball. Distribute the rules (two different sets, randomly shuffled, remember) and instruct participants to read the directions silently, "so that everyone can concentrate." Give everyone a couple minutes to study the rules. Then collect the rule sheets.

☐ Have the participants form two teams, still without talking. (If you have a really large group, you may want to divide into four teams and have two games going on simultaneously.)

☐ Explain where the boundaries are on each side of the "court." Give each team a balloon and have them pass it to their server. (Since both sets of rules specify that the player at the right end of the back row is the server, and since that is the normal place for a volleyball server, this should not cause any confusion.)

☐ Let the play commence. If participants begin to complain about someone not following the rules, say, "*Let's not argue; just play.*" Continue until participants are feeling frustrated because others are not following the rules as they understand them and are arguing in earnest. (Do not, however, let these arguments get out of hand and do not let the game continue too long, as frustrations may get too high.) At some point, someone may say, "I quit." That is all right—it is a normal response to the situation and should be processed along with other responses. If someone threatens to walk out, however, end the game and proceed to "Processing the Game," explaining to that person that an important part of this exercise is letting the group hear how individuals felt in that situation.

Processing the Game (10–30 min.)

☐ Acknowledge that two different sets of rules were handed out before the game commenced.

☐ Then ask the following questions:

1. What was it like for you playing this game? How did you feel? Why

did you feel that way? (At this stage, limit comments to feelings.)
2. Were you more frustrated (angry, etc.) with your own teammates or with the members of the other team?
3. Did the game have any meaning when people were playing with different rules?
4. When did you realize that different participants had been given different rules? How did you feel about that?
5. Was it possible for you to follow the rules you had been given when others were trying to follow other rules?
6. How do you think you would have felt had it been really important whether you and your team won or lost?

Input—*Anomie* (10–30 min.)

☐ Ask: *How was the experience of the game like* anomie? This will help you ascertain how well participants understand the concept. If necessary, say: *This game was designed to give everyone a small taste of what it is like when social norms and understandings are changing and people have a sense of meaninglessness. Some people continue living by the old norms, and others live by the new. Some find that it is impossible to follow the rules as they have been given.*

☐ Present as much material from the Participant's Book as is necessary.

Break (10 min.)

(For 2¹/₂–hour sessions)

Bible Study (20–40 min.)

☐ Ask participants to think about *anomie* and how people respond to it as someone reads aloud (or summarizes) the reflections on Nehemiah 5:1–19, on pages 80–81 in the Participant's Book. Then ask a volunteer to read or summarize Nehemiah 5:1–5.

☐ Have participants form four groups, but stay in the same room so everyone can hear the next step. (If your group has fewer than four participants, have each person play a different role of those described below.)

☐ Explain that each group will plan a skit, acting the part of people who lived in Jerusalem at the time of Nehemiah. Each group will illustrate a different response to anomie. In Group 1, one or more persons are to be a "self-blamer"; in Group 2, a "hustler"; in Group 3, a "quitter"; and in

Group 4, a "rebel." Give groups 5 to 10 minutes to prepare. (If you have short sessions, groups may have to discuss how persons in these categories would have responded instead of devising skits to act out. Then move on to the Scripture reading below [Nehemiah 5:6–19].)

☐ Each group should perform its skit in turn.

☐ After all have presented, discuss the following questions. (Focus on questions 1–4 and ask but don't discuss the last three.)

1. How did you feel as you acted out your role, and why?
2. Which responses to the socioeconomic situation were healthier for the individuals involved? Which were less healthy?
3. Which responses were more constructive and had the possibility of making things better?
4. What insights about our contemporary situation did you get from this Scripture and/or from the skits?
5. How would you describe the feelings of those who participated in the protest?
6. As governor of Judah, in what other ways might Nehemiah have responded?
7. Select one of these options and prepare a "might-have-been" skit to show what might have happened next.

☐ Now read Nehemiah 5:6–19. Ask the following questions:

1. What are some elements of the story (including the part we read earlier) that reflect the presence of *anomie?* How do you think Nehemiah's actions impacted the development of *anomie* or helped to alleviate it?
2. What had contributed to the breakdown of a sense of community?
3. Was the "protest" helpful or harmful?
4. What might have happened had Nehemiah "cracked down" on the protestors, instead of listening seriously to their complaints?

Input—Post-traumatic Stress Disorder (PTSD) (15–35 min.)

☐ Summarize or ask someone in the group to summarize the section of the Participant's Book on trauma.

☐ Then have participants form four small groups, and assign each group one of the five questions from page 84 in the Participant's Book. Give the small groups 7 to 10 minutes. Reassemble the total group for reports from small groups.

☐ Ask participants to turn to the story of Kevin Tucker in the Participant's Book and to identify symptoms of PTSD. Ask *What can we learn from this account?*

Action Plan (5–25 min.)

☐ Ask if anyone has an update on an on-going Action Plan activity.

☐ Invite participants to volunteer for Action Plans. If time permits, brainstorm interview questions as a group.

☐ Ask if any participants have devised alternative Action Plans for the group to consider.

Closing (5 min., optional)

☐ Invite participants to help create a litany of prayer for those experiencing *anomie* or PTSD. Agree on a response such as, "God, be with everyone in distress." Let participants mention people or groups for whom to pray and have everyone say the response together.

DOUBLE-BALLOON VOLLEYBALL

Directions: Read the rules silently.
When you have finished, raise your hand.

RULES

1. Double-balloon volleyball is played with two balloons. The person at the right end of the back row of players is the first server. Each server must serve from that position by hitting or throwing the balloon.

2. When the leader blows a whistle, both servers try to hit the balloon over the net. Two other players on the server's team may assist in helping the balloon over the net if the serve did not carry it far enough.

3. Every player on the receiving team must touch the balloon before hitting it back over the net.

4. When the balloon hits the floor on one side of the net, the team on the other side gets a point. Play continues without a pause until both balloons are on the floor.

5. When both balloons are on the floor, the player who served the previous time selects whomever he or she wishes to be server for the next round. These two players exchange positions; all other team members remain in the same position. The whistle is blown again, and play resumes.

Double-Balloon Volleyball

Directions: *Read the rules silently.*
When you have finished, raise your hand.

Rules

1. Double-balloon volleyball is played with two balloons. The person at the right end of the back row of players is the first server. Each server must serve from that position by hitting or throwing the balloon.

2. When the leader blows a whistle, both servers try to hit the balloon over the net. One other player on each team can hit the balloon on over the net if the server did not hit or throw the balloon far enough.

3. No more than two players on a team may touch the balloon before it goes back over the net.

4. When the balloon hits the floor on one side of the net, the team on the other side gets a point. Play continues without a pause until both balloons are on the floor.

5. When both balloons are on the floor, the person to the left of the server moves into serving position. Other players rotate in the direction of the serving position, with the previous server going into the row closest to the net. The whistle is blown again, and play resumes.

SESSION 7

ECONOMIC JUSTICE AND YOUTH VIOLENCE

FACILITATOR PREPARATION

The game entitled "These Are the Breaks" is a key learning tool for this session. It should be ordered well in advance from the author (see Introduction, page xvi). It is priced to cover just the cost of production and postage. If you use the game during this session, use the session plan that comes with it in place of this one.

"These Are the Breaks" may be played in the session, or you might arrange in-home "parties" at which participants play and discuss it before the session. If you neglected to order it in time for this session, you may still order it and arrange to play it later, as a reinforcement of what is learned.

Make posters with the quotes by Allan Creighton and Paul Kivel, by Father Greg Boyle, and by Roy L. Honeycutt.

You may wish to get a copy of *Amazing Grace: The Lives of Children and the Conscience of a Nation* from a bookstore or library and to read some of the material omitted from the excepts in the Participant's Book.

You can decide whether or not to read some of this additional material during the session if you are not playing "These Are the Breaks."

For Interfaith Groups or Groups Not Related to the Church

If you are not using the Scripture text, extend the reflection on the excerpts from *Amazing Grace* or reflect on the boxed story by Carl Upchurch, discussing the relationship between individual values and socioeconomic realities. Read the excerpt from poem, "Aner Clute," by Edgar Lee Masters, from the box on page 5 in Session 1. How does it relate to the point Carl Upchurch makes?

Objectives
☐ Participants will participate in a game that illustrates social inequality
☐ Participants will be able to express some relationships between economic injustice and youth violence

Scripture
☐ Micah 2:1–2,8–10

Supplies Needed
☐ Group Binder
☐ One "These Are the Breaks" game for each four to six participants, if you are using it
☐ Posters with the quotations by Allan Creighton and Paul Kivel and by Greg Boyle, written in large letters
☐ Optional: Poster with the quotation by Roy L. Honeycutt in large letters
☐ Bibles or photocopies of the Scripture passage for this session for each participant

SESSION OUTLINE
Check-in (10–20 min.)
☐ Ask participants to pair off with someone they did not pair up with during the previous session and share highlights of what they learned from an Action Plan they worked on or from relevant TV or radio programs or newspaper articles—or something that they have experienced or been thinking about since the last session. Each participant will have 2 minutes. When 2 minutes are up, ask the second person in each pair to share.

☐ Have everyone return to the large circle. Take 8 to 10 minutes to give those who want to share an opportunity to do so.

☐ Make sure reports of Action Plan actions are put in the Group Binder.

Input (15–40 min.)
☐ **Option 1:** If you have ordered the game designed for this session,

"These Are the Breaks," play it now, and use the discussion questions that came with it.

□ **Option 2:** Have someone read aloud the excerpts from *Amazing Grace: The Lives of Children and the Conscience of a Nation* by Jonathan Kozol, which are on page 97 in the Participant's Book. If you obtained the book, you may want to read additional excerpts that were not provided in the Participant's Book. Discuss the reflection questions provided in the Participant's Book.

Break (10 min.)
(For 2¹/₂–hour sessions)

Bible Study (15–35 min.)
□ Give a brief introduction to the biblical text in Micah, drawing on the material in the Participant's Book and any other resources on Micah that you may have.

□ Divide into small groups. Have participants turn in their Bibles to Micah 2:1–2,8–10. Ask a good reader to read this passage aloud while everyone follows along, listening carefully.

□ Ask each group to

    1. List specific actions criticized by Micah

    2. Compare the different translations or versions of the passage being used by various participants (Omit this step if you have a short session.)

    3. Discuss what current forms of injustice Micah might attack were he to speak in our country or state today

□ Ask each group to make a poster together. Select some verse or verses from the reading to paraphrase in modern English. Use it on your poster. Draw symbols or pictures with markers to illustrate the verses you paraphrase and the modern forms of injustice you think Micah would oppose.

□ As each group posts its poster, have one member of that group explain it to the larger group.

□ If the following issues did not arise in the discussion, you may wish to ask: *Were Micah to appear in the United States today, what would he say about the fact that 20 percent of our children live beneath the poverty line? About the high level of child abuse in this country? About racism and prejudice? About the wide disparities of expenditures per pupil on various school districts in the same state?*

Discussion (5–20 min., optional)

☐ Post the quotations by Creighton and Kivel and by Boyle.

☐ Divide participants into two groups (or as many small groups as seems appropriate for the number of participants). Assign one group to discuss the quote by Creighton and Kivel and the other group to discuss the quote by Boyle.

☐ Say: *Discuss this quotation in light of our study and especially this session. What do you think the writer(s) wanted to communicate? How do you respond to the statement? What implications does it have for us as we work to eliminate youth violence? Select someone to report the highlights of your discussion to the whole group.*

☐ Return to the circle and ask a spokesperson from each group to share highlights of their discussion.

Action Plan (15–30 min.)

☐ Ask for updates on on-going Action Plan activities.

☐ Ask: *What would we like to know about social and/or economic justice in our own state and/or community?* List the responses on newsprint.

☐ Brainstorm possible sources of information: *Whom might we interview? What information can we find from the newspaper, the police department, department of children's services, human rights commission, the Internet, etc.?*

☐ If you have time left, brainstorm some interview questions. Otherwise, ask for volunteers to formulate interview questions and conduct interviews and for other volunteers to follow up on other kinds of information.

Closing (5–10 min., optional)

☐ Ask participants to meditate silently as you read the quotation from Gandhi several times. Read it slowly and pause for 60 seconds between each of your readings.

☐ If you wish, close with sentence prayers.

SESSION 8

THROW ALL THE BOYS IN THE NILE– RACISM AND YOUTH VIOLENCE

FACILITATOR PREPARATION

If you are using the text from Exodus, it would be helpful to read the whole story of Joseph in Genesis 37–50.

If you can get up-to-date statistics on expenditures on individual school districts in your state, make a large graph comparing districts with the highest and lowest expenditure per child and the district or districts serving your community. If you can't get such numbers for your own community, graph the statistics found on pages 106–107 in the Participant's Book.

Cut paper dolls for the "Racism and the Justice System" activity. Make and use a pattern so all the dolls will be identical except for color, each one as large as a sheet of construction paper, so there will be room to write on it. For every four dolls cut from white or cream paper, cut one from brown paper. This provides for an approximation of the ratio of European Americans and African Americans in the U.S., and of the ratio of European American to African American drug users.

If your sessions are only one hour, you need two sessions to cover the material in this chapter. If that is impossible, concentrate on "Inequalities in Education" or "Racism and the Justice System"; don't try to cover both. There may be some objection to the discussion of the justice system in relation to drug laws and drug law enforcement. Be prepared to ask questions such as, "Is telling people to quit using drugs like telling homeless people to get jobs? Is it fair for drug use to be treated as a medical issue in some neighborhoods and as a criminal issue in others? Should people who use drugs be treated the same, regardless of where they live and the color of their skin?"

Objectives

☐ Participants will be able to express ways in which racism is institutionalized in America
☐ Participants will discuss applications of Exodus 1:8–22 to issues of race, justice, and gangs in the U.S. today

Scripture

☐ Exodus 1:8–22

Supplies Needed

☐ Group Binder
☐ Bibles
☐ Newsprint
☐ Colored markers
☐ Graph showing disparities in school funding
☐ Optional: "Paper dolls" cut from construction paper, enough for all participants

For Interfaith Groups or Groups Not Related to the Church

You may use the text from the Hebrew Scripture and relate it to other incidents of the intentional destruction of other populations, such as the Holocaust. Or substitute reflection on "The Color of Justice." Reflection questions are in the Participant's Book.

SESSION OUTLINE
Check-in (15–25 min.)

☐ Ask group members to form pairs. State: *Take turns sharing what you have learned and thought about since the last session. You will each have 2 minutes to talk. I will tell you when the first person's time is up. During your partner's time, don't interrupt; just listen.* Set a timer. After 2 minutes ask the second person (in each pair) to begin.

☐ After the group has checked in with their partners, have everyone pull their chairs back into the circle, and ask, *Who would like to share with the group what you have learned or been thinking about since last time?* Take up to 20 minutes for this discussion.

Bible Study (15–20 min.)

☐ Read the first paragraph from Session 8 in the Participant's Book. Then ask someone to read Exodus 1:8–22. Depending on the group, it may be necessary to ask only two of the questions, "What do you see happening in the text?" and "In what ways is it parallel to what is happening to persons of color, especially young African American males, in the United States today?" Or, ask the questions on pages 104–105 in the Participant's Book.

☐ Add the following questions at appropriate times: *What are some of the contributions of African Americans and other "minority groups" to life in the United States that have been "forgotten" by many people?* If the group is not able to respond to these questions, ask, *What does our inability to answer these questions suggest?*

☐ Ask: *What are some benefits European Americans deny to themselves and the rest of the nation by denying people of color a fair and equal chance? What are some ways in which dominant elements in the U.S. exert control over the poor and persons of color? What can you do to help see to it that a generation of people of color are not thrown into the Nile of poor schools, gangs, or prisons?*

Inequalities in Education (25–35 min.)

☐ Explain that now the group is going to look at the issue of racism and its connection to youth violence and gangs. You will begin by working in small groups.

☐ Divide into groups of about five to seven participants and give each group colored markers and a sheet of newsprint.

☐ Give these directions: *Brainstorm a description of the kind of school you want to attend, or would want your children to attend. Use prose, poetry, or art to depict this school.*

☐ When the groups have finished, ask them to come up with a slogan to print on their newsprint, such as, "Good Schools Help Keep Children from Being Thrown in the Nile of Hopelessness." Have someone from each group post that group's newsprint and briefly explain something about it.

☐ Now, post and explain the graph showing discrepancies in educational spending per child in various districts.

☐ Ask participants the following questions:

1. What is your reaction to this data?

2. How would you (or do you) feel if your child were (or is) consigned to a substandard school where he or she could not (or cannot) get a decent education? How would you feel if your children had windowless classrooms shared with other classes, or if they were taught by a string of substitutes because they did not have regular teachers for the year?

3. What are you willing to do keep children from being thrown into a Nile of despair and hopelessness due to poor schools?

☐ Finally, read the quotation from Jonathan Kozol in the box on page 107 in the Participant's Book and ask for comments.

Racism and the Justice System (25–45 min.)

☐ Have participants form seven groups or pairs and assign each group one of the following stages possible in the "case study" described below. (If you don't have enough participants for seven, omit stage 6; if that is still too many, either give each group more than one stage or select others to omit.)

1. Police officers see teen in park or on the street and suspect him of drug use.

2. Police officers take teen into custody and escort him to headquarters.

3. Teen is arrested and the district attorney determines what charges to file.

4. Court-appointed attorney for the teen meets with the D.A. to attempt a plea bargin.

5. The case goes to trial, with a European American judge and jury hearing the case.

6. The teen (defendant) is found guilty of possession of cocaine, his third felony conviction.

7. The imprisoned teen requests a drug rehabilitation program.

☐ Give each group one brown and four white or cream-colored paper dolls. Ask each group to let their paper dolls represent teenage boys. Say: *Using the discussion in the Participant's Book for guidance, write a scenario for each of the cut-outs, representing a likely outcome if that young person were at the stage of the criminal justice system to which I will assign your group.* The scenario should be written on the appropriate paper dolls.

☐ When each group is finished, ask them to post their "dolls" with the scenarios. Post those with a positive outcome—the teen is allowed to go home, is put in drug rehab, allowed to plea bargain, etc.—on one wall, and those with a negative outcome on another wall, which should be labeled "The Nile." On each wall, post the scenarios in the order of the group stage number (e.g., Stage 1, Stage 2, etc.).

☐ Say: *Let's walk around the room and read the scenarios. When you are finished reading, you may take your seat in the circle.*

☐ When everyone is seated, ask: *Who is willing to share how you felt as you did this exercise and as you read the scenarios? To what extent do you think the scenarios were realistic? Did they reflect the data given in the Participant's Book? Were some "wishful thinking"?*

☐ Then ask, *What part of the picture we have constructed together on the wall needs to be changed to be more realistic? What part of the reality of this situation needs to be changed to be more just? What are some ways we can work to bring about needed changes?*

Race, Class, and Youth Violence (5–10 min.)

☐ Share the following story:

When Colleen Thompson, a teacher of Conroe, Texas, wanted to introduce a lesson on prejudice and discrimination, she marked each child's hand with an X or an O when they entered the classroom. For a time, she only called on the X's. She complimented the X's and made statements implying that the O's weren't very smart. Later, she switched, and said it was really the O's who were smarter, and asked them to tutor the X's. She reported, "I was frankly shocked by the strength of their anger, and by how their anger focused internally.... It only took about three minutes until the children with the 'wrong mark' on their hand realized they were being discriminated against and began to tune out on the lesson, try to change the mark on their hands from the one the teacher had given to the mark of the favored group, and to begin getting angry."[1]

☐ Ask: *If prejudice and discrimination can create this impact in 3 minutes, how might a steady diet of it impact a person? How might this dynamic relate to youth violence and/or to gang membership?*

Break (10 min.)
(For 2½–hour sessions)

Race and White-Supremacy Gangs (10 min., optional)
☐ Reflect on this section, using some or all of the questions found on pages 114–115 in the Participant's Book.

Action Plan (15–20 min.)
☐ First, ask if anyone needs help or encouragement with an on-going Action Plan activity. Allow participants to respond to one another if questions or concerns are raised.

☐ There are many possible Action Plans suggested for this session. Ask participants to scan the list. Ask them which ideas they want to follow up on. List the names of volunteers and the plan they will work on.

Closing (5 min.)
☐ Say: *I am going to read two paragraphs from an article. As we listen, let's think about the ways in which racism affects the children we are willing to throw, figuratively, into the Nile.*

> Although juvenile crime is down, media reports give a strikingly different impression. The spate of highly publicized school shootings in the past year—in Springfield, Ore.; Fayetteville, Tenn.; Edinboro, Pa.; Jonesboro, Ark.; West Paducah, Ky.; and Pearl, Miss.—showed America a category of youth violence rarely aired on the six o'clock news: White students shooting and killing other White students.
>
> According to Pepperdine University's National School Safety Center in Westlake Village, Calif., killings at schools have fluctuated: there were 55 in the 1992–93 school year; 25 for 1996–97, and 41 for 1997–98. However, in the eight months since the school killings began last October, Vincent Schiraldi, director of the Justice Policy Institute, estimates that 900 Black youth were killed in the United States. No media blitz surrounded that statistic.[2]

☐ You may wish to close with a prayer circle, giving participants an opportunity to voice a prayer of repentance or commitment.

Notes
1. *Colleen Thompson, "On the Other Hand,"* Teaching Tolerance 4:2 *(Fall 1995), 56–57.*
2. *Victoria Valentine, "Youth Crime, Adult Time,"* Emerge *(October 1998), 50.*

SESSION 9

POVERTY, RACE, AND INTERNALIZED OPPRESSION

FACILITATOR PREPARATION

Study the Scripture passage with your cofacilitator(s). Gather the supplies listed on page 55. It will be helpful to the group if you print in large letters on newsprint the two sets of questions for pairs used the Introduction section.

In preparation for the next session, find out if any of the participants have read the books by Luis Gonzalez, Nathan McCall, or Sanyika Shakur (a.k.a. Monster Kody Scott). If so, ask if those individuals are willing to make a presentation on the life of the author during Session 10. Ask them not to focus on the lurid details of some of these men's actions, but to emphasize the factors that led them to become involved in violence and those which influenced them to turn to more constructive lifestyles. The length of time you have for these reports will depend on how many of them you have, the length of your session, and whether or not you are using one of the recommended videos.

For Interfaith Groups or Groups Not Related to the Church

If you are not using the biblical material, substitute reflection on the poem by Nellie Wong.

SESSION OUTLINE
Check-in (15-25 min.)

☐ Ask participants to pair off and share highlights of what they learned or have been thinking or doing since the last session. Allow each participant 2 minutes. Ask each pair to decide who will speak first and tell the first person to begin. When 2 minutes are up, ask the second person to share.

☐ Have everyone return to the large circle. Take 10 to 15 minutes to give individuals an opportunity to share. Make sure no one dominates the time.

☐ Ask everyone to turn in material for the Group Binder.

"The Joke's on Me" (5-10 min.)

☐ Ask someone to read aloud the first three paragraphs of "The Joke's on Me" from page 120 in the Participant's Book.

Objectives

☐ Participants will be able to define "internalized oppression" and "internalized racism"
☐ Participants will list evidences of oppression and of internalized oppression in the biblical story
☐ Participants will discuss the relationship between internalized oppression and some expressions of youth violence

Scripture

☐ Exodus 2:11–15; Numbers 11:4–6

Supplies Needed

☐ Group Binder
☐ Newsprint and markers (or chalkboard and chalk)
☐ Paper and one pencil or pen for each participant
☐ Newsprint with questions for the "Power Relationships" activity
☐ Bibles

☐ Then ask: *In what ways can you identify with this story? What positive or negative messages have you been given about "people like you"? How have these messages impacted you?*

"Power Relationships" (15-30 min.)

☐ Ask participants to turn to "Power Relationships" on page 119 of the Participant's Book. Read the introductory material at the top together. Then ask participants to circle the terms in the columns labeled "Power" and "Nonpower" that apply to themselves.

☐ Ask participants to listen carefully to the following directions, not beginning until all the directions have been read: *Select* **one** *category you circled in the nonpower group. On a piece of paper, list stereotypes or negative statements you have heard directed at that group. For instance, if you select the category of youth, you may have heard someone say, "Kids today don't have respect for anyone." If you circled only words on the power list, think of yourself during childhood or teen years and respond on the basis of what you remember from that period of your life.*

☐ When everyone is finished, ask participants to get in groups of three and count off, so they will know who will start.

☐ Post the questions prepared on newsprint for the participants' reference. Then state: *Each of you will have 2 minutes to share your response to these questions.* (Time each participant and ask that others not interrupt.)

  1. How did you feel as you did this exercise?

  2. What category of which you are a member is subjected to the most bias and/or discrimination?

  3. In what ways have you internalized some of the stereotypes or negative statements you have heard about this group? How have they impacted your life?

☐ Gather everyone in the large group. Repeat the questions above and ask participants to share their responses. Allow for discussion.

Bible Study (20–40 min.)

☐ Summarize the discussion of internalized oppression from page 120 in the Participant's Book. This may be a new concept for some participants. Ask for questions.

☐ Introduce the Bible study by explaining: *The biblical passage for this session follows one that was read in Session 1. The Hebrew people were oppressed by the Egyptians. They had arrived in Egypt as free people, welcomed by the government. Now, however, the Egyptians perceived them to be a threat. The Hebrews were enslaved and made to work for the Egyptians. As the Hebrew population continued to grow, the Egyptians felt more and more threatened. As you may remember from Session 8, the Egyptian government called for the drowning of Hebrew boy babies to stem this population growth.*

☐ Post three sheets of newsprint—one labeled "Power Relationships," one labeled "Oppression," and the last labeled "Internalized Oppression." Ask someone to read Exodus 2:11–15.

☐ Draw a line down the middle of the "Power" sheet. Label one column "Power" and the other "Nonpower."

☐ Ask: *What are some power relationships that existed during the time the Hebrews were in ancient Egypt?* List responses appropriately under the headings of "Power" and "Nonpower." The group may go beyond the text to include gender and age relationships, but be sure that "master/slave" and "Egyptian/Hebrew" are included in the list.

☐ Ask: *What evidences of oppression do you see in this passage?* List these responses on the newsprint labelled "Oppression."

☐ Ask: *What evidences of internalized oppression do you see?* Record responses on the "Internalized Oppression" sheet. Then ask: *If the Hebrews have internalized their oppression, what are some other ways— not evident in this particular text—in which it might have been expressed?* Add these to the list, perhaps using a different-color marker.

Break (10 min.)
(For 2¹/₂–hour sessions)

Youth Violence, Gangs, and Internalized Oppression (25–40 min.)

☐ Have participants briefly review the story of Nathan McCall.

☐ Ask: *What power relationships are involved? Chart the responses on newsprint.* (While dealing with this question, you may want to include age relationships as well as racism and classism.)

☐ Then ask the following questions:

1. What might be some relationships between internalized oppression and youth violence?

2. Which of the "toxic" elements of culture that we discussed earlier do you find in this story?

3. What elements in this story suggest that *anomie* might be developing?

☐ Ask someone to read the quotation by Luis Rodriguez (page 127 in the Participant's Book). Then ask for comments. If no one else mentions it, you may want to note that gang violence—especially among gangs in minority or poverty-stricken neighborhoods—is most often directed toward members of the same ethnic group who belong to a different gang. By internalizing oppression, persons devalue their own ethnic group. In contrast, white hate groups target others—people of color, Jewish and Muslim people, gay men and lesbian women. These supremicists have internalized the misinformation of white supremacy and feel justified in targeting groups that have been devalued by cultural biases.

☐ Ask: *If internalized oppression is one key to youth violence or other negative gang behaviors, what are some changes that need to be made in order to alleviate these problems?*

Action Plan (10–20 min.)

☐ Ask if anyone needs help with an ongoing Action Plan activity, or has a long-range Action Plan to propose.

☐ Ask for volunteers who are willing to undertake the Action Plans proposed for this session.

Closing (5 min., optional)

☐ Ask everyone to listen thoughtfully as you (or one of the participants) read the poem by Nellie Wong on page 121 in the Participant's Book. Follow it with a moment of silent reflection.

☐ If you wish, close with this prayer: *Creator God, we know you created each person on earth with equal value. Help us each to value ourselves and to value all other human beings. Cleanse our hearts of both prejudice and internalized oppression so that we may be fully human and recognize the humanity of others. Amen.*

SESSION 10

GRACE OR JUDGMENT? PREVENTION, INTERVENTION, OR PUNISHMENT

FACILITATOR PREPARATION

Read through the Participant's Book for Session 10 before reading the Session Outline that follows.

If participants agreed to report on books by Gonzalez, McCall, or Shakur (Scott) as described in the Facilitator Preparation section of the previous session plan, check to be sure those volunteers will be ready. Remind them of the recommended foci, and let them know how much time they will be given (depending on the length of your session and the number of reports). If no one has volunteered and if you have not gotten one of the videos to show, one or more facilitators should be prepared to report on these books.

If you did not obtain one of the recommended videos, give more time to these reports and for discussion of the stories of Gonzalez, McCall, and Shakur. Be sure to relate them to the four positive approaches to youth violence (Resource 2).

Make a photocopy of Resource 5 for each participant.

Objectives

☐ Participants will be able to identify characters from the Bible who acted in a violent way but received the call of God

☐ Participants will be able to explain the approaches to youth violence described in Resource 2 and to indicate which approach or approaches could be adopted by their group

☐ Participants will commit themselves to continued action on the issue of youth violence

Scripture

☐ Exodus 2:11–16 and/or Acts 7:54—8:1; 9:1–2

Supplies Needed

☐ Group Binder

☐ Optional: One of the recommended videos

☐ Bibles

☐ Newsprint and markers

☐ Photocopies of Resource 5, from page 52 in the Participant Book

For Interfaith Groups or Groups Not Related to the Church

If you do not use the Scripture, spend more time reflecting on the videos and/or reports on the books, and on planning.

SESSION OUTLINE
Check-in (12–20 min.)

☐ Ask participants to pair off with someone they haven't paired up with recently and share highlights of what they learned through an Action Plan or something they have been thinking of regarding youth or youth violence. Each participant will have 2 minutes to share. Let them know when 2 minutes have elapsed, and ask the second person in each pair to share. Ask that participants listen attentively and not interrupt their partners.

☐ Have everyone return to the large circle. Take 8 to 10 minutes to provide for sharing and discussion. Make sure that no one dominates the time.

☐ **Optional:** Divide into pairs again. Give the pairs 3 minutes to discuss the following questions: *If a person has committed a violent act, is it possible to rehabilitate that person, or is he or she a "lost cause," someone who must be permanently removed from society? What do you think about the philosophy of "three strikes and you're out"? In other words, should a person convicted of three felonies automatically be given a life sentence?*

Bible Study (10–20 min.)
(For 2¹/₂–hour sessions)

☐ Divide participants into groups of three to eight persons, depending on the size of your group. Assign half the groups Exodus 2:11–15 concerning Moses (a passage that should be familiar from Session 9) and half, Acts 7:54—8:1 and 9:1–2 concerning Saul. (Alternatively, you may let each group decide which to study.)

☐ Ask each group to read the relevant Scripture passage, discuss the following questions, and be prepared with a short report.

1. How do you view the violence in this story?

2. How do you think it was viewed by the witnesses? By government and/or religious authorities? By the friends of the victim? By the biblical text?

3. Should Moses/Saul have been jailed or given the death penalty for what he did?

☐ After discussing these questions, the groups should turn to Deuteronomy 34:8–12 (re: Moses) or 1 Corinthians 1:1–2 and 15:1–11 (re: Saul/Paul), and discuss how the later actions of this person impact their viewpoint on how/whether the earlier violence should have been treated.

☐ Give each group a brief time to report on its study. If more than one group studied the same character, ask one group to report and allow the others to add anything else they feel is significant.

☐ Ask: *Does anyone have any general reactions to the Bible study that they would like to express? Do these stories change your thinking about the possibility of rehabilitation of those who are violent or of the possibility that someone who has committed acts of violence as a young person will be able to make positive contributions to society? How did you respond to the stories of more contemporary people in the Participant's Book?*

Is There Life after Crime and Violence? (45–60 min.)

☐ **Step 1:** Divide participants into four groups. Assign each group to one of the following sections of Resource 2 (pages 10–14 in the Participant's Book): "Healing of Violence," "Prevention," "Intervention," "Public Advocacy." Ask each group to read and briefly summarize the relevant section of Resource 2. Provide newsprint and markers with which they can record key points.

☐ **Step 2, Option 1:** Show one of the videos, *Youth Struggling for Survival* or *Gangs Turning the Corner* (or as much of the video as you have time for). Then, divide into the same four groups and give each group these questions:

1. What ideas in the video impressed you most?
2. Which ideas in the video fall into the category to which your group was assigned? List these on newsprint.
3. Which of these ideas would be most helpful in our community? Put a star by each.
4. What other ideas came to mind as you watched the video?
5. If our group were to adopt the approach to which we were assigned, what one action would we recommend? (Responses to this question can come from among ideas that were portrayed on the video, ideas on the handout, or thoughts resulting from participation in this study.)

☐ **Step 2, Option 2:** Ask the participants who have agreed to present reports on Luis Gonzalez, Nathan McCall, or Sanyika Shakur to do so now. Ask each small group to meet again and answer these questions:

1. What insights do the reports give on the approach to which we were assigned?
2. What actions by community organizations and/or communities of faith might have helped keep these young men from the violence they got involved with?
3. What helped them overcome the violence and negativity in their lives?
4. Which of the ideas we have discussed fit into the category of approaches to which we were assigned?
5. If our group were to adopt the approach to which we were assigned, what one action would we recommend? (Responses to this question can come from among ideas that come from the reports, ideas on the handout, or thoughts resulting from participation in this study.)

☐ Have everyone to return to the circle, and ask each group for a report. Concerning each approach, ask: *What is most difficult about this approach? What makes it difficult? What would be most rewarding? What resources (people and material) would be needed by a group working in this area?*
☐ Finally ask: *To which approaches are we willing to commit?*

Action Plan (15–30 min.)

☐ Form a new set of groups with one representative from each group. Ask each group to negotiate a consensus Action Plan, drawing on the best ideas of the members of the group. Have each group put this Action Plan on newsprint on the wall when they are finished.
☐ Reassemble into one circle, and ask each group for a brief report. Then

ask: *Which goal or goals do you think best represent what we might want to do as a group (congregation, coalition)?* Attempt to reach a consensus on this question. Put the consensus goal (or goals) on fresh newsprint.

☐ Ask: *Who is willing to continue meeting in order to make this plan a reality? What resources (people and material) would be needed by a group undertaking this action? Should we attempt to recruit additional participants or partners from the community for this project?*

☐ Distribute copies of the planning form (Resource 5, on page 52 in the Participant Book). Suggest that each participant fill out a copy as you record decisions on the newsprint. If you have a large group, you may select two or three goals and actions on which to work. If your group is small, you will probably want to complete one action before deciding on a new one, though some members may want to be involved in public advocacy while others engage in one of the other approaches.

☐ Depending on the size of your group and the amount of time you have remaining, you may want to negotiate one or more detailed Action Plans, or you may decide to appoint a committee to take the goal or goals agreed on and spell out the rest of the Action Plan, taking into account (but not limited to) the suggestions already on newsprint. You may need to take your plans to the congregational board, pastor, or partner organizations. Decide when to meet to work together on the project(s) selected.

Closing (5–10 min.)

☐ Have the group form a circle. Explain that you will close with a litany celebrating the commitments to stop youth violence and to protect, guide, and love children and youth. Say: *If you are ready to make a commitment, please express your commitment by saying, "As a result of our study, I will … "* and complete the sentence to reflect your personal decision. After each statement, the group will respond, *"God, help us keep our commitments. We want to make a safer world for children and youth."*

☐ When you sense that everyone who wants to make a commitment has done so, you may say or sing *Amen*.

☐ Close by singing "O God of Vision,"[1] if you wish.

Note

1. *Jane Parker Huber,* A Singing Faith *(Philadelphia: Westminster Press, 1987), 17.*